# Marriages Reported by
# DER LIBANON DEMOKRAT

a
German Language Newspaper
Published at Lebanon,
Pennsylvania

Translated and Transcribed
by
*Robert A. Heilman*

HERITAGE BOOKS
2009

# HERITAGE BOOKS
*AN IMPRINT OF HERITAGE BOOKS, INC.*

## Books, CDs, and more—Worldwide

For our listing of thousands of titles see our website
at
www.HeritageBooks.com

Published 2009 by
HERITAGE BOOKS, INC.
Publishing Division
100 Railroad Ave. #104
Westminster, Maryland 21157

Copyright © 1990 Robert A. Heilman

Other books by the author:

*Deaths Reported by* Der Libanon Demokrat, *a German Language Newspaper Published at Lebanon, Pennsylvania, 1832–1864*

*Jacob Ebersoll, the Immigrant of 1763, and His Descendants*

*Marriage and Death Notices Transcribed from the Pages of the* Lebanon Valley Standard

*Marriages Reported by* Der Libanon Demokrat, *a German-Language Newspaper Published at Lebanon, Pennsylvania*

*The Heilman Family Genealogy, Comprising Three Heilman Lines in One Volume: John Peter Heilman (John Peter Heylman); and William B. Heilman and Their Descendants*

*CD: Lebanon Valley, Pennsylvania Marriages and Deaths, 1832-1864*

All rights reserved. No part of this book may be reproduced or transmitted in any form or by any means, electronic or mechanical, including photocopying, recording or by any information storage and retrieval system without written permission from the author, except for the inclusion of brief quotations in a review.

International Standard Book Numbers
Paperbound: 978-1-55613-361-9
Clothbound: 978-0-7884-8200-7

Foreword

Der Libanon Demokrat was a German language newspaper that was published weekly at Lebanon, Pa. from 1827 to 1865. The paper was started in the year 1827 by John and Joseph Miller as an anti-Mason newspaper and was originally titled Der Libanon County Demokrat. Sometime during the eighteen-thirties they changed the name to Der Libanon Demokrat. Subsequently, it became the voice of the Republican party in Lebanon County. Strangely enough, its inconsistent name endured until the year 1865 when the paper was merged with the Berks County Zeitung and the name was changed to Der Pennsylvanier.

John P. Sanderson, a member of the Lebanon Bar, succeeded the Messrs. Miller as publisher. Just when Sanderson assumed control of the paper is not now known.

In 1851 the paper was sold to John Young and John L. Becker. Young became the editor. This partnership lasted until 1859 when Becker withdrew because of a disagreement over the purchase of a building that would provide larger and better quarters. Becker was replaced by the Honorable J. Henry Miller and John C. Seltzer and on October 18, 1859, the building at Nos. 14 and 16 South Eighth Street was sold by David M. Karmany to Messrs. Young, Miller and Seltzer who then comprised the firm owning Der Libanon Demokrat. The name of the firm was John Young and Co.

About 6 months later, J. Henry Miller withdrew. John Seltzer, who lived at Jonestown, was never active in the firm.

In May of 1865 John Young changed the name of the newspaper to Der Pennsylvanier and Der Libanon Demokrat came to an end.

Despite its existence of 38 years, only random issues are available. No editions have been found for years prior to 1832 and none after the years 1864. The years 1850 to 1854 are well represented and, with the exception of 1854, may be complete or nearly complete. Altogether there are more than 1,000 marriages involving about 2,500 people (brides, groom, and parents) reported in the pages of Der Libanon Demokrat that are currently available to researchers.

I extend my thanks to the personnel of the Lebanon County Historical Society, the Lebanon Community Library and the Pennsylvania State Library for making available to me the existing editions of Der Libanon Demokrat.

MARRIAGES

Der Libanon County Demokrat                    Lebanon, Pa.

April 27, 1832

Married. On last Sunday [April 22], by the Rev. Mr. Curran, Mr. Henry Schaffer with Miss Elizabeth Zweyer, both of Lebanon Township.
On the 19th of this month, by the Rev. Mr. Ernst, Mr. Daniel Epler, of Dauphin County, with Miss Elisabeth Kienpatz of Londonderry Township, Lebanon County.

September 14, 1832

Married. By the Rev. Ernst.
On the 23rd of August, Mr. Adam Weber, with Miss Elisabeth Meily, both of this city [Lebanon].
On the 6th of this month, Joseph Fischhorn, with Miss Maria Longenecker, both of Londonderry Township.
On the day named [September 6], Mr. Samuel Westenberger, with Miss Catharina Becker, both of Lebanon Township.
On last Sunday [Setpember 9], Mr. Johannes Lantz, with Maria Schneider.

Der Libanon Demokrat                           Lebanon, Pa.

February 9, 1838

Married. On the 30th of January by the Rev. Mr. Ulrich, Mr. John Holzstein with Miss Maria Moyer, both of Heidelberg Township, Lebanon County.

May 25, 1838

Married. On the 6th of this month, by the Rev. Mr. Leinbach, Mr. John Westenberger, with Miss Anna Maria Lautermilch, both of Lebanon Township.
On the 10th of this month, by the Rev. Mr. Leinbach, Mr. Andress Gerrett of Reading, to Miss Rebecca Meyer, of Myerstown.
On the 16th of this month, at Oak Dale, Dauphin County, Dr. George Rex of South Bend, Indiana, with Miss Henrietta, daughter of General Thomas Harper.
On the 17th of this month, in Hanover, York County, Levi Klein, Esq., of this city [Lebanon], to Miss Bellamina Ebert, of the city of Hanover.

December 14, 1838

Married. On the 6th of this month, by the Rev. Mr. Wagner, Mr. Jeremiah Light, with Miss Hannah Elliott, both of East Hanover Township.
On the 9th of this month, by the same [Rev. Wagner], Mr. Daniel Yeagley, with Miss Elisabeth Daub, both of

Der Libanon Demokrat                    Lebanon, Pa.

December 14, 1838 Continued

Swatara.

### December 21, 1838

Married. On the 11th of November, by the Rev. Mr. Leinbach, Mr. Benjamin Peifer, with Miss Louisa Arnold, both of Tulpehocken Township, Berks County.
On the same day [November 11], by the same [Rev. Leinbach], Mr. Isaac Yingst, with Miss Maria Matis, both of Jackson Township, Lebanon County.
On the 24th of November, by the same [Rev. Leinbach], Mr. Jonathan Royer, with Miss Leucetta Stewart, both of Jackson Township.
On the 4th of December, by the same [Rev. Leinbach], Mr. John Gerhard, with the widow Martha Rieth (Reed), both of Heidelberg Township, Berks County.
On the 8th of December, by the same [Rev. Leinbach], Mr. Elias Klopp, with Miss Elisabeth Miller, both of Heidelberg Township, Berks County.
On the 6th of December, by the same [Rev.Leinbach], Mr. Isaac Forrer, with Miss Elisabeth Dornbach, both of Jackson Township, Lebanon County.
On the day named [December 6], by the same [Rev. Leinbach], Mr. Isaac Spang, of Heidelberg, Berks County, with Miss Susanna Miller of Heidelberg, Lebanon County.

### June 5, 1840

Married. On the 30th of May, by the Rev. Mr. Ruthrauff, Mr. James Conrad, with Miss Mary A. Funk of Annville.

### July 16, 1841

Married. On the 7th of June, by the Rev. Mr. Leinbach, Mr. Henry Stager, with miss Elisabeth Litsch, both of Lebanon Township, Lebanon County.
On the 4th of this month, by the same [Rev. Leinbach], Mr. Michael Philip, with Miss Ro. Spengler, both of Jackson Township, Lebanon County.

### August 22, 1845

Married. On the 14th of this month, by the Rev. Mr. Wagner, Mr. David Xander, with Miss Catharina Horst, both of Londonderry Township, Dauphin County.
On the day named [August 14], by the same [Rev. Wagner], John Seider with Miss Elizabeth Wilhelm, both of West Hanover Township, Dauphin County.
On the 17th of this month, by the same [Rev. Wagner], Mr. Jonathan Walter, with Miss Lucetta Reber, both of

Der Libanon Demokrat                          Lebanon, Pa.

## August 22, 1845

South Lebanon Township.
On the 10th of this month, by the Rev. Leinbach, Mr. Andrew Tice, with Miss Elizabeth Shirk, both of Jackson Township.
On the day Named [August 10], by the same [Rev. Leinbach], Mr. John Zeller, with Miss Sarah Schultz, both of Millcreek Township.
On the day named [August 10], by the same [Rev. Leinbach], Mr. Zadock Noll, with Miss Susan Eberly, both of Millcreek, all of Lebanon County.
On the 10th of this month, by the Rev. J. L. Reber, Mr. Daniel Kieffer, with Miss Lydia Anna Spitler, both of Lebanon County.

## December 6, 1846

Married. On the 5th of this month, by the Rev. Mr. Gering, Mr. John Everett, with Miss Sarah Eisenhauer, both of Swatara Township, Lebanon County.
On the 27th of November, by the Rev. Mr. Ernst, Mr. Jacob Springer, of Lancaster County, with Miss Anna Kaufman, of Dauphin County.
On the 29th of last month, by the same [Rev. Ernst], Mr. Daniel Hauk of East Hanover, Lebanon County, with Miss Elisabeth Gingrich, of Dauphin County.
By the Rev. Mr. Leinbach.
For some weeks, Mr. Thomas Fischer, with Miss M. Gerhard, both of Lebanon County.
On the 4th of last month, Mr. Levi Law, with Miss Rebecca Thierwachter, both of Jackson Township.
On the 6th of November, Mr. Abraham Reyer, with Miss Sarah Stager, both of Heidelberg.
On the 13th of November, Mr. Esra Reed, with Miss Catharina Lechner, both of Marion, Berks County.
On the 20th of November, Mr. Samuel Dondor [Dundore], with Miss Ellen Witman, both of Bernville, Berks County.
On the 31st of October, Mr. Adam Newman, with Miss Catharina Palm, both of Millcreek, Lebanon County.
Likewise: Mr. H. Absolom Spatz, with Miss Eliza Fieman, both of Marion, Berks County.
On the 3rd of this month, by the Rev. Mr. Fischer, the Rev. Mr. J. L. Reber, of Jonestown, with Miss Elmina M., daughter of the Rev. Leinbach, of Jackson Township.

## December 25, 1846

Married. On the 17th of this month by the Rev. Ruthrauff, Mr. Jacob Snavely, of North Lebanon, with _____ Eliza Brooks, of Lebanon.

Der Libanon Demokrat                    Lebanon, Pa.

### December 25, 1846 Continued

Married. On last Tuesday [December 22], near Colebrook Furnace, by the Rev. Mr. Gerhart, Mr. Leonard Seltzer, of Londonderry, Lebanon County, with Miss Margaret Porter, of Mount Joy, Lancaster County.

### February 19, 1847

Married. On the 8th of this month, by the Rev. Mr. Wagener, Mr. Daniel Keller, of North Lebanon Township, with Miss Rebecca Maury, of South Annville Township, Lebanon County.

On the 18th of last month, by the Rev. Mr. Wagener, Mr. Michael Bechtel, of Berks County, with Miss Mary Keller, of South Lebanon Township.

On the 25th of last month, by the same [Rev. Wagener], Mr. John Zinn, with Miss Sarah Shimp, both of South Lebanon Township.

On the 29th of last month, by the Rev. Mr. Ernst, John Sebold, with Miss Catharine Anspach, both of South Annville Township.

### May 10, 1850

Married. By the Rev. Mr. Baker.
On the 14th of April, Mr. Archibald Miller, with Miss Catharina Yeager, both of Lebanon.
By the Rev. Mr. Krotel.
On the 28th of April, Mr. William Focht, of North Lebanon Township, with Miss Susanna Unbehacker, of this city [Lebanon].
By the Rev. Mr. Stacher.
On the 5th of this month, Mr. Carl B. Phreaner, of East Hanover, Lebanon County, with Miss Rebecca Walter, of South Hanover, Dauphin County.

### May 24, 1850

Married. By the Rev. J. Hand.
On the 16th of this month, Benjamin Mooney, with Miss Ellen John, both of Cornwall.
On the 16th of this month, Mr. John Witmeyer, with Miss Sarah Ann McLane, both of Cornwall.
On the 19th of this month, Mr. John Schneider, with Miss Elisabeth Benson.

### May 31, 1850

Married. By the Rev. Sand.
On the 9th of May, Mr. Johann Benson, with Miss C. Emrich, both of Lebanon.

Der Libanon Demokrat                        Lebanon, Pa.

### May 31, 1850 Continued

Married. On the 23rd of May, Mr. Johann Miller, of East Hanover, with Miss Maria Wagner of Berks County.
By the Rev. J. L. Reber.
  On the 19th of May, Mr. Peter Klein with Miss Mary Ann Sarge, both of Fredericksburg.
By the Rev. C. A. Hay.
  On the 12th of May, Mr. Henry Witmer with Miss Caroline Smith, both of South Lebanon Township.

### June 7, 1850

Married. By the Rev. J. Kleinfelter.
  On the 2nd of this month, Mr. Samuel Betz, with Miss Mary Elisabeth Engel, both of Lancaster County.
By Peter Stouch, Esq.
  On the 26th of May, Mr. James Conran, with Miss Harriet Peters, both of South Lebanon Township.

### June 14, 1850

Married. By the Rev. Ditzler.
  On the 11th of June, Dr. Samuel R. Bucher, with Miss Katharina E. Illig, both of Schaefferstown.
By the Rev. J. A. Sand.
  On the 6th of June, Mr. Felix Light, of North Lebanon, with Miss Sara Henry, of South Annville.

### June 21, 1850

Married. By the Rev. J. L. Reber.
  On the 13th of June, Mr. William Dieffenbach, of Pinegrove, with Miss Eliza Felty, of Pinegrove Township, Schuylkill County.
By the Rev. H. Wagner.
  On June the 18th, Rev. Daniel Herr, of Ephrata, Lancaster County, with Miss Catharine Snavely, of South Lebanon Township, Lebanon County.
  On June 6th, Mr. Francis Kolb, of Lebanon, with Miss Elisabeth Barwig, of New York.
By the Rev. T. H. Leinbach.
  On the 6th of June, Mr. William Williams, with Miss Anna Cox, both of South Lebanon Township.
By the Rev. Mr. Kremer.
  On the 11th of June, Mr. Jacob Buschong, of Reading with Miss Anna E., daughter of Mr. Markly of Fayetteville, Franklin County.

### June 28, 1850

Married. By the Rev. A. C. Wedekind.

Der Libanon Demokrat	Lebanon, Pa.

### June 28, 1850 Continued

Married. On the 23rd of June, Mr. Adam Moyer, with Miss Susanna Mellinger, both of this city.
By the Rev. Mr. Schelly.
A short time ago, Dr. George W. Ditzler, with Miss Anna Maria Reinhard, both of Pinegrove.
By the Rev. T. H. Leinbach.
On the 20th of June, Mr. Josiah Rothermel with Miss Elisabeth Malthar, both of Myerstown.

### July 5, 1850

Married. By the Rev. J.'M. Hoffmeier.
On the 30th of June, in this city [Lebanon], Dr. Thomas R. L. Ebur of Orwigsburg, with Miss Sebilla Ludwig, daughter of Peter F. Ludwig, Esq., of West Brunswick.

### July 12, 1850

Married. By the Rev. L. Gerhart. On the 18th of June, Mr. John Winkelblech, of Centre County, with Miss Amanda Kinzel of Lebanon County.

### August 2, 1850

Married. By the Rev. A. C. Wedekind.
On the 28th of July, Mr. George Schraum with Miss Eliza Zeller, both of South Lebanon Township.
By the Rev. H. Walsch.
On the 24th of July, in Philadelphi, Mr. John Walsch of Philadelphia, with Miss Lucretia M., daughter of Adam Grittinger, Esq., of this city [Lebanon].

### August 9, 1850

Married. By the Rev. J. L. Reber.
On the 3rd of August, Mr. Tobias Mees, of Union Township, with Miss Sarah Keller, of this city [Lebanon].
By the Rev. Mr. Krotel.
On the 4th of August, Mr. Henry Reichmann with Miss Mary Margaret Schultz, both of this city [Lebanon].
By the Rev. Mr. Stein.
On the 15th of June, Daniel Wolf with Miss Maria Fischer, both of Bethel Township.
On the 23rd of June, Wilhelm Behny, with Miss Elisabeth Boeshore, both of Swatara.
On the 23rd of June, Mr. Henry Behny, of Jackson, with Miss Elisabeth Reifein of North Lebanon Township.
On the 18th of July, George Lang of West Hanover Township, Dauphin County, with Miss Christina Wallmer, of Union Township, Lebanon County.

Der Libanon Demokrat							Lebanon, Pa.

### August 16, 1850

Married. By the Rev. Mr. Krotel.
 On the 11th of August, Mr. John Speitel, of Miami County, Ohio, with Miss Louisa Bene, of Annville, Lebanon County.
 On the 8th of August, Mr. Samuel Matter, with Miss Leah Kitzmiller, both of South Annville Township.
 On the 8th of August, Mr. Samuel Hallman with Miss Hanna Brough, both of North Lebanon Township.
By the Rev. H. Wagner.
 On the 20th of July, Mr. William Hoke with Miss Mary Mees, both of South Lebanon Township.
 On the 8th of August, Mr. John Bischop, with Miss Rebecca Ault, both of Londonderry Township.

### August 23, 1850

Married. By the Rev. Mr. Krotel.
 On the 15th of August, Mr. George Hess with Miss Mary Anna Embich, both of the city of Lebanon.

### August 30, 1850

Married. By the Rev. H. Wagner.
 On the 27th of August, Mr. Cyrus Wittmeyer with Miss Nancy Hostetter, both of South Annville Township.
By the Rev. S. Von Neida.
 On the 15th of August, Mr. John Black, with Miss Sarah Lindenmuth, both of Myerstown.

### September 20, 1850

Married. By the Rev. D. Ulrich.
 On the 25th of August, Mr. Isaac Rieth with Miss Elisabeth Strickler, both of Heidelberg Township.
 On the 12th of this month, Mr. Edward Walborn with Miss Sara Mosser, both of Jackson.
By the Rev. William Pauli.
 On the 1st of this month, Mr. William A. Moyer, of this city [Lebanon], with Miss Angelina Bischop, both of Exeter Township, Berks County.
By the Rev. Mr. Krotel.
 On the 15th of this month, Mr. Jacob Brossman with Miss Sarah Lutz, both of Lebanon County.
 On the 12th of this month, Mr. Henry Hostetter of South Annville, with Miss Nancy Nachtsinger, of Londonderry.
 On the 12th of this month, Mr. Josiah Otzman with Miss Mary Elisabeth Rahn, both of Hummelstown.
 On the 12th of this month, Mr. Washington Leitzel of Berks County with Miss Eliza Gilbert of this city.

Der Libanon Demokrat                    Lebanon, Pa.

                September 27, 1850

Married. By the Rev. S. Von Neida.
  On the 19th of this month, Mr. David Schell with Miss Caroline DeHart, both of Myerstown.
By the Rev. Mr. Krotel.
  On the 22nd of this month, Mr. George Trostel with Miss Catharina Miller, both of North Lebanon.
By the Rev. Mr. Stein.
  On the 19th of this month, in Lancaster, Mr. Cyrus Bachman with Miss Catharina Hoffer, both of South Annville Township.
By the Rev. Mr. Kleinfelter.
  Mr. George Becker with Miss Susanna Greims, both of Millcreek Township.
By the Rev. J. H. Leinbach.
  On the 7th of this month, Mr. John Becker with Miss Catharina Wolf, both of Bethel.
  On the 21st of this month, Mr. John Schaeffer with widow Catharina Morer, of Stouchsburg, both of Berks County.
  On the 24th of this month, Mr. William F. Killinger with Miss Elisabeth Carver, both of Myerstown.

                October 4, 1850

Married. By the Rev. Mr. Krotel.
  On the 26th of September, Mr. Moses McKinney, of South Annville, with Miss Angelina Bleistein, of North Lebanon.
  On the 29th of September, Mr. Levi Schaffer, of Lebanon County, with Miss Rebecca Wagner, of Berks County.
By the Rev. Mr. Hoffmeier.
  On the 26th of September, Mr. John Schreckengast with Miss Mary Buck, of East Hanover Township.
By the Rev. Mr. Scholler.
  On the 19th of September, Mr. Joseph Schnebly with Miss Magdalina Baer, both of Dauphin County.

                October 11, 1850

Married. On the 3rd of this month, in Campbelltown, Mr. John Burkholder with Miss Louisa Wolfersberger, both of Campbelltown.

                October 18, 1850

Married. By the Rev. J. L. Reber.
  On the 15th of October, in Jonestown, Mr. John L. Becker, publisher of Der Libanon Demokrat, with Miss Elizabeth Stein of Jonestown.
  On the 10th of October, Mr. John Hegy, with Miss Re-

Der Libanon Demokrat                           Lebanon, Pa.

October 18, 1850 Continued

becca Peter, both of Annville.
By the Rev. A. C. Wedekind.
   On the 15th of October, Mr. Christian Wiest of Lancaster County with Miss Lydia Hostetter of Jackson Township.
By the Rev. Mr. Krotel.
   On the 10th of October, Mr. Jacob Koons with Mrs. Annie Atlet, both of South Annville Township.
   On the 11th of this month, Mr. John Schuster with Miss Mary Ann Achenbach, of South Lebanon Township.
By the Rev. T. H. Leinbach.
   On the 3rd of October, Mr. Jacob Krick, of Tulpehocken, Berks County, with Miss Caroline Walborn, of Jackson Township.
By the Rev. Mr. Kleinfelter.
   On the 11th of October, Mr. Joseph Meyer, with Miss Sarah Ried, both of Millcreek.

October 25, 1850

Married. By the Rev. Mesick.
   On the 17th of this month, Mr. T. T. Worth, of this city [Lebanon], with Miss Mary Ellen, daughter of Dr. J. Wiestling, of Harrisburg.
By the Rev. H. Wagner.
   On the 17th of this month, Mr. Joseph Blouch, of North Lebanon Township, with Miss Catharine Wittmeyer, of Swatara.
By the Rev. Mr. Stein.
   On the 15th of this month, Mr. Adam Imboden with Miss Leah Carmony, both of Annville.
   On the 10th of this month, Mr. Abraham Stauffer, of Annville, with Miss Catharina Baker, of Rapho Township, Lancaster County.

November 1, 1850

Married. On the 22nd of October, by the Rev. T. T. Yeager, Mr. Henry Stohler, with Miss Catharina Phillippi, both of Lebanon County.
   On the 29th of October, by the Rev. A. C. Wedekind, Mr. John Allison, of North Lebanon, with Miss Amelia Richards, of this city [Lebanon].
   On the 22nd of October, by the Rev. Mr. Stein, Mr. Samuel Umbenhend, with Miss Sarah Weidel, both of Jackson Township, Lebanon County.
   On the 13th of October, by the same [Rev. Stein], Mr. David Kercher of the Monroe iron works, with Miss Elisabeth Keen, of Bethel Township, Lebanon County.
   On the 13th of October, by the Rev. J. Gring, Mr. C.

Der Libanon Demokrat                                    Lebanon, Pa.
              November 1, 1850 Continued

D. M'Cauley, with Miss Lavina Desch, both of Fredericksburg.
    On the 17th of October, by the Rev. J. Hand, Mr. John Scheiner, with Miss Lydia Hornefius, both of North Lebanon.
By the Rev. T. H. Leinbach.
    On the 5th of October, Mr. John Moyer, with Miss Mary Gassert, both of Tulpehocken, Berks County.
    On the 9th of October, Mr. John Yerger, with Miss Sarah Lab, both of Bethel, Berks County.
    On the 11th of October, Mr. Edward Zerbe with Miss Carolina Lutz, both of North Heidelberg, Berks County.
    On the 13th of October, Mr. Joseph Noll, of Heidelberg, with Miss Susanna Zeller, of Millcreek, Lebanon County.
    On the 17th of October, Mr. John Umberger, with Miss Lea Fegle, both of North Lebanon Township.
    On the 25th, Mr. Franklin Filbert, with Miss Mary Forry, both of Tulpehocken, Berks County.
    On the 27th, Mr. Henry Boas, with Miss Magdalena Boas, both of Myerstown.
By the Rev. D. Ulrich.
    On the 9th of October, Mr. John Schaffer, with Miss Lovinia Miller, both of Tulpehocken, Berks County.
    On the day named [October 9], Mr. George Peter Uhrich, of Marion, Berks County, with Miss Henrietta Zeller, of Millcreek, Lebanon County.
    On the 26th, Mr. Isaac Stiely, with Matilda Roths, both of Bern, Berks County.
    On the day named [October 26], Mr. Tobias Hoffman, with Miss Catharina Christ, both of Schaefferstown, Lebanon County.

                        November 8, 1850

Married. On the 3rd of this month, by the Rev. Mr. Reber, Mr. Peter Bensing, with Miss Lea Moyer, both of Bethel Township.
    On the day named [November 3], by the same [Rev. Reber], Mr. Benjamin Schwarz, with Miss Fianna Mutschler, both of Swatara.
    On the 29th of October, by the Rev. Mr. Wedekind, Mr. John Allison, of North Lebanon, with Miss Amelia Richards of this city [Lebanon].
    On the day named [October 29], by the Rev. Mr. Krotel, Mr. Michael Nafzger, of Londonderry, with Miss Mary Ketterline, of South Annville Township.
    On the day named [October 29], Mr. _____ Flowers, of Londonderry, with Miss _____ Kurz, of Derry Township, Dauphin County.

Der Libanon Demokrat                           Lebanon, Pa.

              November 8, 1850 Continued

Married. On the 27th of October, by the Rev. Mr. Bollinger, Mr. Henry Bollinger, with Miss Anna Royer, both of Jackson.
   On the day named [October 27], by the same [Rev. Bollinger, Mr. John Klein, with Miss Leah Herzler, both of Jackson Township.

                  November 15, 1850

Married. By the Rev. Mr. Stein.
   On the 10th of September, Henry Hassinger, of Lewistown, Mifflin County, with Miss Rebecca Dollinger, of Bethel Township.
   On the 26th of September, Mr. Isaac Miller, with Miss Susanna Grumbein, both of Swatara Township.
   On the 3rd of October, Benjamin G. W. Hoffert, with Miss Rebecca Wolf, both of Bethel Township.
   On the 21st of October, Joseph Rittel, with Miss Susanna Gerth, both of North Lebanon.
   On the 26th of October, John Hess, of Union Township, with Miss Catharina Wertz, of East Hanover Township.
   On the 7th of November, Jacob Klein, of Jackson Township, with Miss Hannah Wolf, of Bethel Township.
   On the 10th of November, Samuel Wolf, of Swatara, with Miss Catharina Stickel, of Bethel Township.
   For some time, Mr. John H. Zell, of Union Township, with Miss Sabina Tittel, of West Hanover Township, Dauphin County.
   On the 31st of October, by the Rev. Mr. Fowle, William Howard Drayton, Esq., of Philadelphia, with Miss Harriet, daughter of the late James Coleman, Esq., of Lancaster County.
   On the 9th of this month, by the Rev. Mr. Krotel, Mr. Peter Spang, with Miss Rebecca Bennethum, both of Womelsdorf, Berks County.
   On the 7th of this month, by the Rev. Mr. Wedekind, Mr. Abraham Henry, with Miss Fanny Hollinger, both of Dauphin County.
   On the 3rd of this month, by the Rev. Mr. Gring, Mr. George Hower, of Bethel Township, with Miss Sarah Ann, daughter of David Weber, of Fredericksburg.
   On the 12th of this month, by the Rev. Mr. C. F. Hoffmeier, Mr. John Runkel, with Miss Rosanna Runkel, both of Palmyra.

                  November 22, 1850

Married. On the 30th of last month, by the Rev. J. Gerhart, Mr. J. Hacker, of New Ephrata, with Miss Charlotte, youngest daughter of John Thomas, Esq., of Manheim, Lancaster County.

Der Libanon Demokrat                    Lebanon, Pa.
November 22, 1850 Continued

Married. On the 12th of this month, by the Rev. Mr. C. F. Hoffmeier, Mr. John Runkel, with Miss Rosanna Miller, both of Palmyra.
On the 11th of this month, by the Rev. Mr. Eggers, Mr. Daniel Strack, with Miss Wilhelmina Harper, both of East Hanover.
On the day named [November 11], by the Rev. Wedekind, Dr. W. Smith, with Miss Hannah Care, both of Hummelstown, Dauphin County.
On the 14th of this month, by the same [Rev. Wedekind], Mr. John Hostetter, of Jackson Township, with Miss Sarah Gockley, of Lancaster County.

November 29, 1850

Married. On the 3rd of this month, by the Rev. Mr. Leinbach, Mr. Henry Frank, with Miss Louisa Hummel, both of Jackson.
On the 16th, by the same [Rev. Leinbach], Mr. William Spitler, of Bethel, with Miss Sophia Fischer, of East Hanover.
On the 11th, by the same [Rev. Leinbach], Mr. Conrad Kurtz, with Mrs. Esther Holdri, both of Berks County.
On the 14th, by the same [Rev. Leinbach], Mr. Henry Noll, with Miss Catharina Krall, both of Heidelberg, Lebanon County.
On the 16th of this month, by the Rev. Mr. Ulrich, Mr. Jonathan Wittman, of Myerstown, with Miss Maria Weiser, of Stouchsburg.
On the 17th of this month, by the Rev. Mr. Leinbach, Mr. William M. Missemer, of Millcreek, Lebanon County, with Miss Susanna Zell, of Enterprise, Lancaster County.
By the Rev. William Pauli, on the 6th of this month, Mr. Isaac Goldman, of Lancaster County, with Miss Wilhelmina Ebach, of Lebanon County.
On the 24th of this month, by the Rev. Mr. Wagner, Mr. Samuel Kipp, with Miss Mary Stober, both of Londonderry Township, Lebanon County.
On the day named [November 24], by the same [Rev. Wagner], Mr. William Hartman, with Miss Sarah Moyer, both of Lebanon.
On the 26th, by the same [Rev. Wagner], Mr. David Lehman, with Miss Anna Steiner, both of Londonderry, Dauphin County.

December 6, 1850

Married. By the Rev. Mr. Stein.
On the 14th of October, Mr. Levi Feldy, of Pinegrove, with Miss Lewina Boeshore, of Union Township, both of Schuylkill County.

Der Libanon Demokrat                           Lebanon, Pa.

                 December 6, 1850 Continued

Married. On the day named [October 14], Mr. Wilhelm Pentikuf, with Miss Catharina Maury, both of West Hanover, Dauphin County.
   On the 21st of November, Mr. Johannes Donemeier, with Rebecca Ritter, both of Union Township, Lebanon County.
   On the day named [November 21st], Mr. Josua Miller, with Miss Sarah Walter, both of Jonestown.
   On the 1st of December, Mr. Levi Viehl, with Miss Carolina Hunsicker, both of Bethel Township, Berks County.
   On the 19th of November, in Manheim, Lancaster County, by the Rev. J. Gerhart, Dr. C. J. Schnebely, formerly of Lebanon County, with Miss Ann M. Ensminger, of Manheim.
   On the 24th of November, by the Rev. G. F. Krotel, Mr. Peter Groh, of Bethel Township, with Miss Elisabeth Wenner, of Erie County, New York.
   On the 26th, by the same [Rev. G. F. Krotel], Mr. Amos Krall, with Miss Susanna Schenk, both of Heidelberg Township, Lebanon County.
By the Rev. H. Wagner.
   On the 28th of November, Mr. John S. Bomberger, with Miss Catharina Brubacher, both of South Lebanon Township.
   On the day named [November 28], Mr. Isaac Gingrich, of North Annville Township, with Miss Nancy Yordy, of South Annville Township.
   On the 26th of November, by the Rev. James Sloan, Mr. P. H. Reinhard, the printer of the "<u>Monongahela Republican</u>," formerly of the city of Lebanon, with Miss Elisabeth S. Gordon, youngest daughter of the esteemed James Gordon, both of Monongahela City, Washington County, Pa.
   On last Tuesday [December 3], by the Rev. J. Hand, William M. Breslin, Esq., the printer of the "<u>Lebanon Advertiser</u>," with Miss Sarah Ellen Oves, of this city [Lebanon].

                    December 13, 1850

Married. By the Rev. T. H. Leinbach: on the 28th of November, Mr. Levi Pain with Miss Henrietta Strickler, both of Lebanon County.
   By the Rev. D. Ulrich: on the 23rd of November, Mr. Jonathan Witman of Lebanon County, with Miss Maria Elisabeth Weiser of Stouchsburg - on the 26th, Mr. Aaron Wentzel, of Berks County, with Miss Catharina Kohl, of Millcreek, Lebanon County.
   On the 28th of November, by the Rev. A. S. Leinbach, Mr. Solomon R. Licht [Light], with Miss Catharina Ann Gockley, both of Lebanon Township.
   On the 21st of November, by the Rev. Charles A. Hay, Mr. Michael Bachman, of Lebanon County, with Miss Sarah

Der Libanon Demokrat                           Lebanon, Pa.
              December 13, 1850 Continued

Landis of Dauphin County.
    On the 24th, by the Rev. Mr. Eggers, Mr. Stephen D. Strohman, of Annville, with Miss Priscilla Beck, of East Hanover.
    On the 16th, by the Rev. Mr. Gring, Mr. David G. Ford, with Miss Elisabeth Schuey, both of Union.
    On the 26th, by the same minister [Rev. Gring], Mr. Johann Henrich Schuey of East Hanover, with Miss Sarah Schuey, of Union Township.
    On the 3rd of this month, by the same [Rev. Gring], Mr. Joseph Naftzinger, with Miss Magdalena Herschberger, both of Union.
    On the 5th of this month, by the Rev. Mr. Stein, Mr. George Seider, with Miss Lydia Wendling, both of East Hanover Township.

                    December 20, 1850

Married. On the 5th of this month, by the Rev. Mr. Stein, Mr. John Kelly, with Miss Susanna Eisenhauer, both of Jonestown.
    On the 10th of this month, by the same [Rev. Stein], Mr. Daniel Wallmer, with Miss Maria Boltz, both of North Annville Township.
    On the 15th of this month, by the Rev. G. F. Krotel, Mr. Washington Moyer, of Fredericksburg, Lebanon County, with Miss Susanna German, of Jackson Township, Lebanon County.
    On the 12th of this month, by the Rev. Augustus C. Wedekind, Mr. William Stoever, with Miss Sarah S. Rohland, both of South Lebanon Township.

                    December 27, 1850

Married. On the 1st of this month, in Mount Joy, Lancaster County, by David Schertzer, Esq., Mr. David Long, of Penn Township, 73 years old, with Miss Elisa Herschey, of the city of Manheim, 18 years old.
By the Rev. Krotel.
    On the 19th of this month, Mr. Benjamin Boyer, of North Lebanon, with Miss Sarah Freimoyer, of Reading, Berks County.
    On the 22nd of this month, Mr. Adam Ney, with Miss Susanna Spohn, both of this city [Lebanon].
    On the 19th of this month, by the Rev. H. Wagner, Mr. John Derkes, with Mrs. Elisabeth Lowery, both of this city [Lebanon].
By the Rev. Leinbach.
    On the 30th of November, Mr. William Rohrer, with Miss Carolina Schwartz, both of Bethel Township, Berks County.

Der Libanon Demokrat                                    Lebanon, Pa.

December 27, 1850 Continued

Married. On the 1st of this month, Mr. Foster Biegeman, with Miss Rebecca Blatt, both of Riemstown, Lancaster County.
On the 12th of this month, Mr. George Meiser, of Millcrrek Township, with Miss Ann Eby, of South Lebanon Township.
On the 17th of this month, Mr. John Bechtold, with Miss Elisabeth Schaffer, both of North Lebanon Township.
On the 21st of this month, Mr. John Pott, with Miss Elisabeth Heberling, both of Marion, Berks County.
By the Rev. J. A. Sand.
On the 19th of this month, Mr. Jacob Etter, with Miss Amende Ellenberger, both of Londonderry Township.
On the 6th of this month, by the Rev. Mr. Schultze, Mr. Henry Graff, with Miss Louisa Thomas, both of this city [Lebanon].
On the 12th of this month, by the Rev. Mr. C. A. Hay, Mr. Henry U. Seltzer, of Belleview, with Miss Ann Hacker, of Dauphin County.

January 3, 1851

Married. On the 24th of December, by the Rev. Mr. Wedekind, Mr. William Scweitzer, with Miss Sarah Knoll, both of Annville.
On the 26th of December, by the same, Mr. Noah Rabb, of Dauphin County, with Miss Catharina Fischer, of Annville Township.
On the 23rd of December, by the Rev. Mr. Miles, Dr. Cyrus Gloninger, of this city, with Miss Julia, daughter of the esteemed A. Beaumont of Wilkesbarre.
On the 10th of December, by the Rev. Mr. Gerhart, Mr. George Leineweber, with Miss Anna Witmer, both of South Lebanon.
On the 15th of December, by the Rev. Mr. Gring, Mr. Thomas Walter, of Jonestown, with Miss Elmina Moyer, of Fredericksburg.
By the Rev. Mr. D. Ulrich.
On the 19th of December, Mr. Jacob Bollman, with Miss Anna Royer, both of Schaefferstown, LebanonCounty - on the 21st of December, Mr. Levi Kurtz, with Miss Susanna Bennethum, both of near Womelsdorf.

January 10, 1851

Married. By the Rev. Thomas H. Leinbach, on the 21st of December, Mr. John Sott, with Miss Elisabeth Heberling, both of Marion, Berks County - on the 31st, Mr. Jonathan Spath with Miss Elisabeth Schneider, both of Millcreek, Lebanon County.

Der Libanon Demokrat                          Lebanon, Pa.

January 10, 1851 Continued

Married. On the 25th of December, by the Rev. F. Hodgson, D. D., Rev. James Colder of the China Mission of the Methodist Church, with Miss Ellen G. Winebrenner, daughter of the Rev. J. Winebrenner, of Harrisburg.
On the 24th of December, by the Rev. Mr. Smith, Mr. Jacob P. Kreider, formerly of this city [Lebanon], with Miss Leah Stahl, of Pinegrove.
On the 31st of December, by the Rev. Mr. Wagner, Mr. David Hunsicker, of Swatara, with Miss Lavina, daughter of Mr. John Ely, of this city [Lebanon],
On the 5th of this month, by the Rev. Mr. Krotel, Mr. Daniel Boyer of North Lebanon, with Miss Catharine Karry of Schaefferstown.
On the day named [January 5], by the same [Rev. Krotel], Mr. Joel Hoffman, with Miss Sarah Jung, both of Lebanon.
On the 2nd of this month, by the Rev. Mr. Wagner, Mr. Jacob Bomberger, with Miss Rosanna Smith, both of South Lebanon.
On the 26th of December, by the Rev. J. H. Menges, Mr. William J. Burnside, Principal of the Annville Academy, with Miss G. McPherson, Lancaster County.

January 17, 1851

Married. On the 5th of this month, by the Rev. Mr. Krotel, Mr. William G. Krater, with Miss Catharina Nace, both of Marietta, Lancaster County.
On the 14th of this month, by the same [Rev. Krotel], Mr. Benjamin M. Ingle, of Lancaster County, with Miss Catharina Wenger, of Lebanon County.
On the 9th of this month, by the Rev. John Hein, Mr. Levi Schiffer, formerly of Harrisburg, with Miss Sarah, daughter ofChristian Eschliman, of Fredericksburg, Lebanon County.
On the 27th of December, by the Rev. Mr. Wedekind, Mr. Thomas Rusley, of Philadelphia, with Miss Margareth Braun, of this city [Lebanon].
On the 9th of this month, by the Rev. Mr. Wagner, Mr. Samuel Bleistein, of South Lebanon, with Miss Lea Stager, of North Lebanon.

January 24, 1851

Married. By the Rev. Mr. Krotel.
On the 16th of this month, Mr. John Groh, with Miss Priscilla C. Reiter, both of Jackson Township.
On the day named [January 16], Mr. Henry Schenk, of Tulpehocken, with Miss Elisabeth Groh, of Jackson Township.

Der Libanon Demokrat                          Lebanon, Pa.
                    January 24, 1851 Continued

Married. On the 19th of this month, Mr. Lorenz Neugardt, of Lancaster County, with Miss Magdalena Keener, of Londonderry, Lebanon County.
    On the 16th of this month, by the Rev. Mr. Wedekind, Mr. John Jones, with miss Louisa Wagner, both of Dauphin County.
    On the 23rd of this month, by the Rev. Mr. Sand, the honorable George Smith, with Miss Rebecca Baer, both of Pinegrove, Schuylkill County.

                       January 31, 1851

Married. On the 28th of this month, by the Rev. Mr. G. F. Krotel, Mr. John Stroh, Jr., with Miss Lucetta Carmony, both of Annville, Lebanon County.
    On the 23rd, by the same [Rev. G. F. Krotel], Mr. George Yordy, with Miss Mary Ann Zimmerman, both of West Hanover, Dauphin County.
    On the 23rd, by the Rev. Wedekind, Mr. Daniel Early, with Miss Amada Mart, both of Londonderry, Lebanon County.
    On the 14th, by the Rev. Mr. Rutter, Mr. Benjamin M. Ingle, of Lancaster County, with Miss Catharina Wender, of Lebanon County.

                       February 7, 1851

Married. On the 18th of January, by the Rev. Thomas H. Leinbach, Mr. David Sonnen, with Miss Angelina Carry, both of Jackson Township, Lebanon County.
    On the 18th, by the same [Rev. T. H. Leinbach], Mr. Jacob Dubs, with Miss Eliza Hautz, both of Bethel Township.
    On the 25th, by the same [Rev. Th. H. Leinbach], Mr. Benewell Spangler, with Miss Mary Himmelberger, both of Union Township, Berks County.
    On the 30th of January, by the Rev. Mr. Krotel, Mr. Charles Meily, with miss Sarah Steckbeck, both of North Lebanon.

                      February 14, 1851

Married. By the Rev. John Stein.
    On the 2nd of January, Mr. John Kniesel of Jonestown, with Miss Amende Hess, of Union Township, Lebanon County.
    On the 11th of February, Mr. John Dubs, of Bethel Township, with Miss Maria Lau, of Jackson Township.
    On the 4th, Mr. Nathaniel Hartlein, with Miss Susanna Huber, both of Jonestown.
    By the Rev. Mr. Wagner, on the 13th of this month, Mr. John F. Schaffner, of North Annville, with Miss Lydia

Der Libanon Demokrat                                Lebanon, Pa.

February 14, 1851 Continued

Ann Fortna, of North Lebanon Township.

February 21, 1851

Married. By the Rev. Mr. Eggers.
On the 4th of this month, Mr. John G. Carmany, of Annville Township, with Miss Frances N. Landis, of Middletown.
On the 16th of this month, Mr. Christopher Bauman, with Miss Hannah Plaugh, both of Londonderry Township.
By the Rev. Mr. Krotel.
On the 6th of this month, Mr. Isaac Wolf, with Miss Matilda Lindenmuth, both of Myerstown, Lebanon County.
On the 16th of this month, by D. W. Leeds, Esq., Mr. Isaac Betz, with Miss Sophia Leininger, both of Millcreek Township, Lebanon County.

March 7, 1851

Married. By the Rev. Mr. Krotel, on the 27th of February, Mr. Moses Early, with Miss Polly Ramler, both of Dauphin County.
On the day named [February 27], by the same, [Rev. Krotel], Mr. Abraham Bartolet, with Miss Elisabeth Hastler, both of Lebanon County.
On the 27th of February, Mr. Levi Uhler, of this city, with Mrs. Ann Weasy, of Manheim, Lancaster County.
On the 2nd of this month, Mr. John Dietrich, with Miss Mary Kline, both of North Lebanon Township.
On the 27th of February, by the Rev. C. F. Hoffmeier, Mr. M. Washington Books, with Miss Mary Reese, both of East Hanover Township, Lebanon County.
On the 1st of May, by the same [Rev. C. F. Hoffmeier], Mr. Isaac Dubs, with Miss Sebilla Boeshore, both of Bethel Township, Lebanon County.
On the 2nd of this month, by the same [Rev. C. F. Hoffmeier], Mr. George Wagner, with Miss Catharina Grumbein, both of Bethel Township, Lebanon County.
On the day named [March 2], by the same [Rev. C. F. Hoffmeier], David Herring, of Jonestown, with Miss Louisa Bender, of Union Township, Lebanon County.

March 14, 1851

Married. On the 6th of this month, by the Rev. Thomas H. Leinbach, Mr. George Allbrecht, of Schaefferstown, Lebanon County, with Miss Maria Weidner, of Bethel, Berks County.
On the 6th of March, by the Rev. Mr. Sand, Mr. Abrm.

Der Libanon Demokrat                          Lebanon, Pa.

             March 14, 1851 Continued

Miller, with Miss Magdalena Miller, both of South Lebanon.
    On last Tuesday [March 11], by the Rev. Mr. Krotel,
Mr. Tobias Reinoehl, with Miss Emma L. Negley, both of
this city [Lebanon].
    On the 6th of this month, by the Rev. Mr. Van Nieda,
Mr. Augustus Steiner, with Miss Susanna, daughter of Daniel Meyer, both of Myerstown.

                March 21, 1851

Married. On the 2nd of this month, by the Rev. Mr. Zug,
Mr. Benjamin Royer, with Miss Mary Weith, both of Jackson Township, Lebanon County.
    On the 6th of March, by the Rev. Mr. Sand, Mr. Abrm.
Miller, with Miss Magdalena Gingerich, both of South Lebanon.
    On the 11th of this month, by the Rev. Mr. Krotel,
Mr. John Graiglow, with Miss Susan Embich, both of this
city [Lebanon].
    On the 18th of this month, by the Rev. Mr. Grop, Mr.
Samuel Licht [Light], with Miss Catharina Wolf, both of
South Lebanon.
    On the 18th of this month, by the Rev. Mr. Reber,
Mr. Milton Cooper, with Miss Mary Meily, both of Mt. Nebo,
Lebanon County.
    On the 15th, by the same [Rev. Reber], Mr. John Daub,
of Jackson, with Miss Catharina Mutschler, of Bethel.

                March 28, 1851

Married. On the 6th of this month, Mr. MOrris Fuchs, with
Miss Sarah Weik, both of Swatara Township.
    On the 18th of this month, Mr. Amos Fuchs, with Miss
Harriet Gelebach, both of Swatara Township.
    On the 18th of this month, by the Rev. J. Wenger,
Mr. Moses Klein, of North Lebanon Township, with Miss
Leah Royer, of Heidelberg Township.
    On the 16th of this month, by the Rev. L. G. Egger,
Mr. Israel Kremer, with Miss Elisabeth Siegrist, both of
Londonderry Township.
    On the 20th of this month, Mr. Henry Spohn, with
Miss Phrany Lawery, both of this city [Lebanon].
By the Rev. Mr. Krotel.
    On the 25th of this month, Mr. Daniel Henning, with
Miss Maria Ziegler, both of Mt. Union, Lebanon County.
    On the day named [March 25], Mr. George Moltz, of
Middletown, with Miss Rebecca Ziegler, of Mount Nebo,
Lebanon County.

Der Libanon Demokrat					Lebanon, Pa.

### April 4, 1851

Married. On the 20th of March, by the Rev. H. Wagner, Mr. Henry Hoke, with Miss Mary Killian, both of South Lebanon.
    On the 25th of March, by the Rev. Thomas J. Yeager, Mr. Daniel Bingeman, of Elisabeth Township, Lancaster County, with Miss Susan Plattenberger, of Lebanon County.

### April 11, 1851

Married. On the 5th of this month, by the Rev. G. F. Krotel, Mr. Jacob Phillips, with Miss Melinda Geiss, both of Jackson Township, Lebanon County.
    On the 30th of March by the Rev. J. L. Raber, Mr. Mahlon Faber, with Miss Catharine Ackerman, both of Jonestown.

### April 18, 1851

Married. On the 8th of March, by the Rev. Mr. John Gring, Mr. Heinrich Hummel, of Pinegrove Township, with Miss Salome Bretzius, of Wann Township, Schuylkill County.
    On the 3rd of April, by the same [Rev. Gring], Mr. William Martin, of East Hanover, Dauphin County, with Miss Susanna Maulfair, of Annville, Lebanon County.
    On the 5th of this month, by the same [Rev. Gring], Mr. Samuel Ehler, with Miss Louisa Zimens, both of Wann Township, Schuylkill County.

### April 25, 1851

Married. (By the Rev. John Stein.)
    On the 22nd of March, Mr. Heinrich Glick, with Miss Sophia Meily, both of Bethel Township, Lebanon County.
    On the 23rd, Mr. George Weidel, with Miss Melinda Bender, both of Union Township.
    On the 25th, Mr. Heinrich Stock, with Miss Lea Miess, both of Hanover Township.
    On the 27th, Mr. John Daub, with Miss Catharina Walmer, both of Union Township.
    On the 10th of April, Mr. Johannes Freiling, with Miss Sarah Zimmerman, both of Londonderry, Lebanon County.
    On the 20th of this month, by the Rev. Mr. Krotel, Mr. Henry Alleman, with Miss Leah Scheib, both of North Lebanon.
    On the 12th of this month, by the Rev. Mr. Wedekind, Mr. John Walter, with Miss Margaret Keltner, both of North Lebanon.
    On the 11th of this month, by the Rev. T. H. Leinbach, Mr. John Smith, with Miss Justina Riem, both of Lebanon County.

Der Libanon Demokrat				Lebanon, Pa.
					May 16, 1851

Married. On the 11th of this month, by the Rev. G. F. Krotel, Mr. Peter Miller, of Reading, with Sophia Klind, of Lebanon.
On the day named [May 11], by the same [Rev. Krotel], Mr. Cyrus Palm, with Miss Elisabeth Getts, both of Lebanon.
On the 13th of this month, by the same gentleman [Rev. Krotel], Mr. Joseph Westenberger, with Miss Phrene Hostetter, both of South Annville Township.
On the day named [May 13], by the same [Rev. Krotel], Mr. John Witman, with Miss Ann Eversole, both of Dauphin County.
On the 3rd of this month, by the Rev. Mr. Gerhart, Mr. Theodore Irisch, with Miss Mary Schaffer, both of East Wicconisco, Dauphin County.
On the 4th of this month, by the Rev. J. L. Reber, Mr. Solomon Miess, with Miss Magdalena Kreiser, both of Union Township.
On the 8th of this month, by the Rev. G. F. Krotel, Mr. Hugh Black, with Miss Leah Boyer, both of Lebanon County.

					May 23, 1851

Married. On the 13th of this month, by the Rev. A. J. Leinbach, Mr. John Ziegler, of Myerstown, Lebanon County, with Miss Mary Zweizig of Reading.
On the 15th of this month, by the Rev. G. F. Krotel, Mr. David Gerberich, of East Hanover Township, with Miss Carolina Stump, of Union Township.
On the 20th of this month, Mr. Samuel U. Schirk, merchant, of this city, with Miss Malinda, daughter of Mr. Pharis Cassidy, formerly of the city of Lebanon.

					May 30, 1851

Married. On the 22nd of this month, by the Rev. Mr. Wedekind, Mr. Levi Heilman, of North Lebanon, with Miss Catharina Focht, of North Annville.
On the 25th of this month, by the Rev. Aaron S. Leinbach, Mr. Moses L. Bauman, merchant, with Miss Maria Ann Muth, both of Lebanon County.
On the 15th of this month, by the Rev. Jacob Adams, Mr. John Kleinfelter, of Heidelberg Township, Lebanon County, with Miss Elisabeth Behm, of Annville Township, Lebanon County.
On the 27th of this month, by the Rev. Mr. Gross, Mr. H. C. Harper, merchant of this city, with Miss Mary A. Hammer, daughter of Mr. Elijah Hammer, of Pottsville, Schuylkill County.

Der Libanon Demokrat                    Lebanon, Pa.

### June 13, 1851

Married. On the 5th of this month, by the Rev. John Stein, Mr. William Gelbach, with Miss Sarah Wagner, both of Fredericksburg, Lebanon County.
    On the day named [June 5], by the Rev. John Gring, Mr. Amos Walmer, with Miss Rebecca Ann Miller, both of Fredericksburg, Lebanon County.

### June 20, 1851

Married. On the 15th of this month, by the Rev. F. W. Kremer, Mr. William Eckert, with Miss Polly Licht [Light], both of North Lebanon.
    On the day named [June 15], by the same [Rev. Kremer], Mr. Joseph Sayler, with Miss Lydia Schally, both of Swatara Township, this county.
    On the 12th of this month, by the Rev. J. Hand, Mr. William Foy, with Miss Sarah Fessler, both of Cornwall.
    On the day named, by the same, Mr. Elias Buchter, with Miss Sarah Donley, both of Cornwall.
    By the Rev. Conrad Miller, Mr. Samuel Behny, of Myerstown, with Miss Amanda Slicher, of Montgomery County.
    On the 8th of this month, by the Rev. G. F. Krotel, Mr. Devilla Bender, of Jackson Township, with Miss Sibilla Black, of North Lebanon Township.
    On the day named [June 8], by the same [Rev. Krotel], Mr. George Preis, with Miss Elisabeth Kurr, both of Jackson Township, Lebanon County.

### June 27, 1851

Married. On the 19th of this month, by the Rev. J. Hand, Mr. Daniel Phreaner, with Miss Susan Atkins, both of this city.
    On the 22nd of this month, by the Rev. F. W. Kremer, Mr. Henry Snavely, with Miss Rebecca Landis, both of Heidelberg Township, this county.

### July 4, 1851

Married. On the 8th of June, by the Rev. T. H. Leinbach, Mr. John Helwig, with Miss Ellen Dall, both of Bethel Township.
    On the 9th of June, by the same [Rev. T. H. Leinbach], Mr. William Moyer, with Miss Sarah Hauert, both of Marion Township.
    On the 19th of June, by D. B. Leeds, Esq., Mr. John Ried, with Mrs. Catharina Guth, both of Millcreek Township, Lebanon County.

Der Libanon Demokrat                    Lebanon, Pa.

July 11, 1851

Married. (By the Rev. Mr. Stein.)
On the 1st of May, Mr. Wilhelm Roth, with Miss Susanna Bader, both of Hanover, Lebanon County.
On the 6th of May, Mr. Joel Fuchs, of Swatara, with Miss Sarah Wagner, of Bethel Township.
On the 8th of June, Mr. Christopher Ulrich, with Miss Elisabeth Baumgartner, both of Hanover Township.
On the 14th of June, Mr. Jacob Ruh, with Miss Anna Maria Kreiser, both of Union Township, Lebanon County.
On the 19th of June, Mr. John Bolz, with Miss Amende Wendling, both of Jonestown.

July 18, 1851

Married. On the 22nd of June, by the Rev. Gring, Mr. George Lauser, of Jonestown, with Miss Leah Peters, of Fredericksburg.

July 25, 1851

Married. On the 20th of this month, by the Rev. Mr. Krotel, Mr. John Leineweber, with Miss Carolina Lauser, both of South Annville.
On the day named [July 20], by the same [Rev. Krotel], Mr. Conrad C. Focht, with Miss Margaret Ann Armstrong, both of Lebanon.
On the 17th of this month, by the Rev. Wedekind, Mr. John Strohman, with Miss Maria Walter, both of South Lebanon.
On the 20th of this month, by the Rev. Mr. Kremer, Mr. Adam Steins of Lebanon, with Miss Sarah Bicher, of South Lebanon.

August 1, 1851

Married. On the 28th of July, Mr. John Epling, with Miss Elisabeth Schneider, both of Palmyra, Lebanon County.
On the 27th of July, by the Rev. G. F. Krotel, Mr. John Borgner, with Miss Julianna McCloud, both of Lebanon.
On the 19th of July, by William Klein, Esq., Mr. Joseph Bibee, with Miss Isabella Helwood, both of Lebanon County.

August 15, 1851

Married. On the 7th of this month, by the Rev. S. von Nieda, Mr. Cyrus Heffelfinger, with Miss Diana Schneider, both of Myerstown.
On the 10th of this month, by the Rev. Mr. H. Schrop,

Der Libanon Demokrat                    Lebanon, Pa.

### August 15, 1851 Continued

Mr. Johann Blouch, with Miss Polly Schort, both of North Lebanon.

On the 12th of this month, by the Rev. F. W. Kremer, Mr. John Schneider, of South Lebanon, with Miss Sarah Schepler, of JOnestown, Lebanon County.

On the 10th of this month, by the Rev. G. F. Krotel, Mr. Peter Weber, of Myerstown, with Miss Catharina Steger, of South Lebanon Township, Lebanon County.

On the 12th of this month, by the same, Mr. Henry Marquart, of Campbelltown, with Miss Mary Seaman, of East Hanover Township, Lebanon County.

### August 22, 1851

Married. On the 7th of this month, by the Rev. T. H. Leinbach, Mr. Levi Meyer, with Miss Matilda Etris, both of Bethel Township.

On the day named [August 7], by the same [Rev. Leinbach], Mr. Friederich Braun, with Miss Mary Schumacher, both of Union Township, Lebanon County.

On the 11th of this month, by the same, Mr. Daniel Wagner, with Miss Lydia Kerchner, both of Jonestown, Lebanon County.

### August 29, 1851

Married. (By the Rev. Mr. Stein.)

On the 22nd of July, Mr. Jacob Reifein, with Miss Maria Grohman, both of Jackson Township.

On the 29th of July, Mr. Jacob Heim, with Catharina Kaufman, both of Jonestown.

On the 31st of July, Mr. Heinrich Ulrich, with Miss Sarah Hauer, both of Behtel Township.

On the 17th of August, Mr. Johann Meyer, with Elisabeth Wagner, both of Bethel Township.

On the 21st of this month, by the Rev. G. F. Krotel, Mr. Henry Preis, with Miss Rebecca Dehart, both of Myerstown.

On the day named [August 21], by the same [Rev. Krotel], Mr. John Schnabeley, of Cornwall, with Miss Mary Ann Sargent, of Annville.

On the 21st of this month, by the Rev. A. C. Wedekind, Mr. Joseph Kochler, with Miss Amanda Fox, both of North Lebanon.

On the 26th of this month, by the Rev. F. W. Kremer, Mr. Daniel Dickel, with Miss Catharina Treite, both of North Lebanon.

On the 21st of this month, by the Rev. J. Hand, Mr. John Schay, with Miss Elisabeth Ferry, both of this city.

On the 17th of this month, by the Rev. T. H. Lein-

Der Libanon Demokrat                    Lebanon, Pa.

August 29, 1851 Continued

bach, Mr. Henry Noll, with Miss Rebecca Seibert, both of Jackson Township, Lebanon County.

September 3, 1851

Married. On the 2nd of this month, by the Rev. Mr. F. W. Kremer, Mr. Abraham Witmer, of Dauphin County, with Miss Elisabeth Overholzer, of Lebanon County.

On the 26th of August, by the Rev. T. H. Leinbach, Mr. John Arnold, with Miss Angelina Stauch, both of Womelsdorf, Berks County.

On the 31st, Mr. Jacob Strack, of Jackson, Lebanon County, with Miss Elisabeth Walborn, of Bethel, Berks County.

On the 2nd of this month, by the same, Mr. Uriah B. Stewart, Esq., of Millcreek, Lebanon County, with Miss Maria Kehl, of Upper Heidelberg, Berks County.

On the 28th of August, by the Rev. J. Adams, Mr. Abraham Artz, of Spring Township, Berks County, with Miss Maria Kleinfelder, of Millcreek, Lebanon County.

September 12, 1851

Married. On the 4th of this month, by the Rev. G. F. Krotel, Mr. Henry McLauglin, of South Lebanon, with Miss Mary Scheiner, of North Lebanon.

On the 28th of August, by John Immel, Esq., Mr. Henry Schwanger, of North Lebanon, with Miss Henrietta Engelhart, of Jackson.

On the 4th of this month, by the Rev. T. H. Leinbach, Mr. Peter Umbenhend, with Miss Matilda Hanefius, both not far from this city.

September 26, 1851

Married. On the 21st of this month, by the Rev. G. F. Krotel, Mr. Elijah Resch, with Miss Leah Beckley, both of Jackson Township, Lebanon County.

On the 15th of this month, by the Rev. C. H. Hay, Mr. Adam Faust, with Miss Eliza Henry, both of Annville, this county.

On the 18th of this month, by the Rev. J. T. Strein, Mr. Moses Hagy, of Penn Township, Lancaster County, with Miss Lucy Ann Long, of Annville, this county.

October 3, 1851

Married. On the 9th of September, by the Rev. Mr. Ditzler, Mr. Edward Eba, of Heidelberg Township, with Miss Rebecca Moyer, of Millcreek Township.

Der Libanon Demokrat                    Lebanon, Pa.

On the 18th of September, by the Rev. Christian Siegrist, Mr. John Weber, of Rapho Township, Lancaster County, with Miss Sarah Ness, of Schaefferstown, Lebanon County.

October 10, 1851

Married. On the 7th of this month, in Hummelstown, by the Rev. Mr. Suhter, Mr. John Yordy, of this city, with Miss Carolina Elisabeth Baum, of Hummelstown.
On the 28th of September, by the Rev. Daniel Ulrich, Mr. Joseph Royer, of Schaefferstown, this county, with Miss Lavina Rieth, of Marion Township, Berks County.
On the 18th of September, by the Rev. J. F. Mesick, Mr. John H. Killwell, of Campbelltown, with Miss Elisabeth Licht [Light], of Hummelstown, Dauphin County.
On the 28th of September, by the Rev. Mr. Leinbach, Mr. William Steiner, of Jackson Township, this county, with Miss Catharina Benetch, of Cocalico, Lancaster County.
On the 25th of September, by the same [Rev. Leinbach], Mr. Craiglow, with Miss Mary Fiess, both of South Lebanon Township.
On the 30th of September, by the Same, Mr. George Mock, with Miss Rosyann Corner, both of Schaefferstown, this county.
On the 2nd of this month, by the Rev. F. W. Kremer, Mr. David Long, with Miss Lidia Ensminger, both of South Lebanon Township.
On the 2nd of this month, by the Rev. G. F. Krotel, Mr. Joseph Gingrich, of North Annville, with Miss Elisabeth Reist, of South Annville Township.
On the 5th of this month, by the Rev. A. C. Wedekind, Mr. Philip Herman, of Dauphin County, with Miss Lydia Ellinger, of North Lebanon.

October 17, 1851

Married. On the 5th of this month, by the Rev. H. Romig, Mr. Solomon Stein (son of the Rev. Stein), with Miss Rebecca Weis, both of Hanover, Lebanon County.
On the 11th of September, by the same [Rev. H. Romig], Mr. Samuel Bolz, with Miss Elisabeth Fenstermaker, both of Lebanon County.
On the 9th of this month, by the Rev. F. W. Kremer, Mr. Henry Forney, with Miss Susan Weltmer, both of Derry Township, Dauphin County.
On the 9th of this month, by the Rev. G. F. Krotel, Mr. David K. Landis, of Derry Township, with Miss Catharina Strubenhauer, of North Annville.
On the 15th of this month, by the Rev. L. G. Eggers,

Der Libanon Demokrat                    Lebanon, Pa.

October 17, 1851 Continued

Mr. John Yuengst, of Derry Township, with Miss Elisabeth Braun, of East Hanover Township, Dauphin County.
 On the 2nd of this month, by the Rev. T. H. Leinbach, Mr. William Wike, of Millcreek Township, Lebanon County, with Miss Rebecca Roth, of Lancaster County.
 On the 2nd of this month, by the Rev. William Gerhardt, Mr. Wesley Quigley, of Lebanon County, with Miss Elisabeth Kurtz, of Dauphin County.

October 24, 1851

Married. On the 7th of this month, by the Rev. J. S. Herman, Mr. William Meyers, of Myerstown, with Miss Lydia H. Forney, of Maiden Creek, Berks County.
 On the 15th of this month, by the Rev. F. W. Kremer, Mr. William J. Burnside, principal of the Annville Academy, with Miss Elisabeth, daughter of Dr. G. Fahnestock, both of Annville, Lebanon County.
 On the 8th of this month, by the Rev. A. C. Wedekind, Mr. Edward Rohland, with Miss Mary Lechner, both of Womelsdorf, Berks County.
 On the 21st of this month, by the same [Rev. Wedekind], Mr. William Altenderfer, of this city, with Miss Rosanna Wittmeyer, of South Lebanon.
 On the 16th of this month, by the Rev. G. F. Krotel, Mr. Amos Deininger, with Miss Lydia Blauch, both of North Annville.
 On the 19th of this month, by the same, Mr. Levi Leob, with Miss Mary Fox, both of Jackson Township.
 On the day named [October 19], by the same [Rev. G. F. Krotel], Mr. Cyrus Wolf, with Miss Carolina Katz, both of Myerstown.
 On the day named [October 19], by the same [Rev. Krotel], Mr. William Forry, with Miss Sarah Lehman, both of Jackson.
 On the day named [October 19], by the same [Rev. Krotel], Mr. David T. Werner, with Miss Sarah Groh, both of South Lebanon Township.
 On the 16th of this month, by the Rev. J. C. Becker, Mr. David B. Gingrich, of South Annville Township, with Miss Sarah Funk, of North Lebanon Township.

October 31, 1851

Married. On the 11th of September, by the Rev. Mr. Stein, Mr. Benneville Lerch, with Miss Maria Mecklindy, both of North Annville Township.
 On the day named [September 11], by the same [Rev. Stein], Mr. Samuel Walmer, with Miss Amanda Braun, both of Londonderry Township.

Der Libanon Demokrat　　　　　　　　　　　Lebanon, Pa.

October 31, 1851 Continued

On the 18th of September, by the same [Rev. Stein], Benjamin Himmelberger, with Miss Christina Kircher, both of East Hanover Township, Lebanon County.

On the 23rd of September, by the same [Rev. Stein], Mr. Heinrich Schuey, with Miss Sarah Steiner, both of West Hanover, Dauphin County.

On the 2nd of October, by the same [Rev. Stein], Johannes Walmer, with Wilhelmina Klemenz, both of North Annville Township.

On the 18th of October, by the same [Rev. Stein], Johannes Gehret, with Leah Ihrig, both of Bethel Township, Berks County.

On the 19th, by the same [Rev. Stein], Mr. William Bricker, of Jackson Township, with Allemina Rittel, of Bethel Township.

On the 21st of October Emanuel Spannuth, with Lydia Trautman, both of Jackson Township.

On the 27th of this month, by the Rev. A. S. Leinbach, Mr. Jacob Hibschman, of North Lebanon, with Miss Henrietta Schwob, of South Lebanon, Lebanon County.

On the 26th of this month, by the Rev. F. W. Kremer, Mr. Abraham Licht [Light], of Bethel Township, with Miss Catharina Hoover, of this city.

On the 23rd of this month, by the Rev. A. C. Wedekind, Mr. Herman Flower, with Miss Elisabeth Gerhard, both of Londonderry Township.

On the day named [October 23], by the same [Rev. A. C. Wedekind], Mr. William Schirk, of Jackson Township, with Miss Sarah Bomberger, of Lancaster County.

November 7, 1851

Married. On the 30th of October, by the Rev. F. W. Kremer, Mr. Andrew R. Henry, with Miss Barbara Forney, botth of Derry Township, Lebanon County.

On the 2nd of this month, by the Rev. G. F. Krotel, Mr. Emanuel Weik, of Heidelberg Township, Berks County, with Miss Amelia Stover, of Lebanon County.

November 14, 1851

Married. On the 7th of October, Rev. Gideon Weidman, of Ephrata, Lancaster County, with Miss Sarah Meass of Schaefferstown.

On the 4th of this month, by the Rev. A. S. Leinbach, Dr. Daniel Hochstetter, of Jackson Township, Lebanon County, with Miss Matilda Deppen, of Heidelberg Township, Berks County.

On the 9th of this month, by the Rev. Thomas Leinbach, Mr. Christian K. Gingrich, of Swatara Township,

Der Libanon Demokrat                    Lebanon, Pa.

November 14, 1851 Continued

with Miss Elvina Fischer, of Marion Berks County.
On the 2nd of the preceding month, by the same, Mr. William Whike, with Miss Rebecca Roth, of Heidelberg, Lebanon County.
On the 4th, by the same, Mr. Ruben Stands, with Miss Christina Moyer, both of Berks County.
On the 21st, in Lancaster City, Mr. Adam Ruth, with Miss Catharina Riem, both of Riemstown [Reamstown], Lancaster County.
On the 26th, by the same, Mr. John Etris, with Miss Maria Gerhart, both of Bethel Township.
On the 6th of this month, by the same, Mr. Aaron Brown, of Jackson, with Miss Elmeina Schott, of South Lebanon.
On the 19th of the preceding month, by the Rev. Mr. Zehring, Mr. Philip Trautman, with Miss Rebecca M'Cormick.
On the 8th of this month, by the same, Mr. William Lebo, with Miss Elisa Deck.
On the day named [November 8], by the same [Rev. Zehring], Mr. Michael Lengel, with Miss Levia Gasser, all of Tulpehocken, Berks County.
On the 6th of this month, by the Rev. Wedekind, Mr. Tobias Stover, with Miss Sarah Ann Kreider, both of South Lebanon.
On the 6th of this month, by the Rev. Hand, Mr. Moses H. Albert, with Miss Maria E. Landis, both of Hanover.
On the 6th of this month, by the Rev. Kremer, Mr. Joseph Umberger, of North Lebanon, with Miss Barbara Corry, of South Lebanon.
On the 13th of this month, Mr. William Murrey, of Union Forge, with Miss Willemina, daughter of Mr. Samuel Bickel, of Jonestown, Lebanon County.

November 21, 1851

Married. On the 6th of this month, by the Rev. Christian Siegrist, Mr. George Phillippi, with Miss Mary Ann Forry, both of Heidelberg Township.
On the 13th of this month, by the Rev. C. Klein, Mr. Henry Zimmerman, of Lebanon County, with Miss Catharina Kuhns, of Dauphin County.
On the 15th of this month, by the Rev. Tho. H. Leinbach, Mr. Isaac Wagner, with Miss Leah Miller, of Upper Tulpehocken, Berks County.
On the day named [November 15], by the same [Rev. T. H. Leinbach], Mr. Henry Etris, with Miss Carolina Hess, both of Tulpehocken, Berks County.

Der Libanon Demokrat                           Lebanon, Pa.

### November 21, 1851 Continued

On the 13th of this month, by the Rev. Mr. Kremer, Mr. Michael L. Schenk, with Miss Maria Hunsberger, both of Conewago Township, Dauphin County.

On the day named [November 13], by the same [Rev. Kremer], Mr. John P. Umberger, with Miss Catharina G. Schaffer, both of this city.

On the 13th of this month, by the Rev. G. W. Hutter, Mr. Samuel B. Lehman, of Lebanon County, with Miss Elisabeth Goodman, of Philadelphia County.

On the 13th of this month, by the Rev. G. F. Krotel, Mr. Samuel Biecher, with Miss Carolina Bender, both of Lancaster County.

On the day named [November 13], by the same [Rev. G. F. Krotel], Mr. Samuel Felter, with Miss Catharina Schenk, both of Lancaster County.

On the day named [November 13], by the same [Rev. G. F. Krotel], Mr. Martin Funk, with Miss Sarah Smith, of Lebanon County.

### November 28, 1851

(By the Rev. Mr. Stein.)
Married. On the 6th of this month, Mr. David Hunsicker, with Miss Elisabeth Licht [Light], both of Bethel Township.

On the 9th of this month, Mr. David Braun, with Miss Susanna Zimmerman, both of Bethel Township.

On the 10th of this month, Mr. Let Rapp, with Miss Maria Kreiser, both of Union Township.

On the 13th of November, Mr. Daniel Zimmerman, with Miss Sarah Rab, both of East Hanover Township.

On the 6th of this month, Mr. John Webert, with Miss Anna Maria Groff, both of Bethel Township.

On the 20th of this month, by the Rev. Mr. Kremer, Mr. David G. Miller, of this city, with Miss Anna, daughter of Mr. John Kleiser, of South Lebanon.

### December 5, 1851

Married. On the 27th of November, by the Rev. Daniel Schrop, Mr. Joseph Licht [Light], with Miss Catharina Kochendorfer, both of North Lebanon Township.

On the 27th of November, by the Rev. G. F. Krotel, Dr. Joseph O. Schindel, with Miss Leah Smith, both of Lebanon.

On the 20th of November, by the Rev. Henry G. Stecher, Mr. Richard Fox, of Hummelstown, with Miss Rachel Ann Patten, of Harrisburg.

Der Libanon Demokrat               Lebanon, Pa.

December 12, 1851

Married. On the 27th of November, by the Rev. Mr. Stein, Mr. Samuel Neu, of Hanover, with Catharina Schnewley, of Annville, Lebanon County.

On the 30th, by the same [Rev. Stein], Jacob Kaufman, of Annville, with Maria Anna Lescher, of Jonestown.

On the 4th of this month, by the same, John Heinrich Schaud, with Elisabeth Kniesel, both of Jonestown.

On the 6th, by the same, Benjamin Schneider, with Eva Lohr, both of Union Township.

On the 7th, by the same, Daniel Tobias, with Relena Bolz, both of Swatara Township.

December 19, 1851

Married. On the 25th of November, in Hamilton, Ohio, by the Rev. Mr. Darling, Mr. John W. Killinger, Esq., of this city, with Miss Mary A., daughter of Dr. Hittle of the first place.

On the 2nd of this month, by the Rev. Mr.L. G. Eggers, Mr. George Daubert, of Union Township, with Miss Eliza Walmer, of East Hanover Township.

On the 4th of this month, by the same [Rev. L. G. Eggers], Mr. Henry Hemperly, of Londonderry Township, with Miss Mary Ann Riehm, of East Hanover Township.

On the 4th of this month, by the Rev. Heinrich Schrop, Mr. Gideon Light, of North Lebanon, with Nancy Witmeyer, of Swatara Township.

On the 11th of this month, by the Rev. F. W. Kremer, Mr. George Hitz, of South Lebanon Township, with Miss Leah Null, of Derry Township, Dauphin County.

On the 16th of this month, by the Rev. Mr. Krotel, Mr. John Stanley, with Miss Priscilla Krause, both of this city [Lebanon].

December 26, 1851

Married. On the 23rd of this month, by the Rev. F. W. Kremer, Mr. Henry Smith, of Berks County, with Miss Carolina Ruhl, of South Lebanon.

On the 9th of October, by the Rev. E. W. Hutter, Mr. Daniel Embich, of Lebanon, with Miss Louisa Smith, of Philadelphia.

On the 25th of August, by the same [Rev. Hutter], Dr. Michael C. Kreitzer, with Miss Mary A. White, both of Myerstown, Lebanon County.

January 2, 1852

Married. On the 25th of December, by the Rev. Henry Schrop, Mr. Johannes Thoma, with Miss Sarah Bonawitz, both

Der Libanon Demokrat							Lebanon, Pa.

January 2, 1852 Continued

of Pinegrove, Schuylkill County.
On the 23rd of December, by the Rev. A. C. Wedekind, Mr. John H. Krick, with Sarah E. Licht [Light], both of this city [Lebanon].
On the 25th of December, by the Rev. G. F. Krotel, Mr. Andreas Braun, of South Lebanon Township, with Miss Sarah Cassel, of Dauphin County.
On the day named [December 25], by the same [Rev. Krotel], Mr. William Bischop, of East Hanover, with Miss Sophia Schirk, of Londonderry Township, Lebanon County.

January 9, 1852

Married. On the 21st of December, by the Rev. C. Siegrist, Mr. Samuel Krumlauf, of Elizabethtown, Lancaster County, with Miss Catharina Loose, of Heidelberg Township.
On the 6th of January, by the Rev. Henry Schrop, Mr. Gideon Blauch, with Miss Rebecca Fernsler, both of North Lebanon Township.
On the 1st of this month, by the Rev. J. Hand, Mr. Samuel Yocum, with Miss Harriet Biemerderfer, both of Schaefferstown, Lebanon County.
On the 4th of this month, by the same [Rev. J. Hand], Mr. Charles Derr, with Miss Louisa Haak, both of Lebanon.
On the 7th of this month, by the Rev. John Gring, Mr. Elijah Moore, of the Monroe iron works, with Miss Elisabeth Gettel, of Fredericksburg.
On the 25th of December, by the same [Rev. Gring], Mr. John Wagner, Jr. of Fredericksburg, with Miss Mary Paine, of Bethel.
On the same day, by the Rev. J. Stein, Mr. John Behny, with Miss Catharina Anspach, both of the Monroe iron works, Lebanon County.

January 16, 1852

Married. On the 6th of this month, by the Rev. J. Hand, Mr. Theodore Oves, with Miss Matilda M., daughter of Mr. William Atkins, both of this city [Lebanon].
On the 11th of this month, by the Rev. G. F. Krotel, Mr. Henry Smith, with Miss Mary Ann Immel, both of Myerstown.
On the 14th of this month, by the same [Rev. G. F. Krotel], Mr. Jacob Philips, with Miss Rachel Fox, both of East Hanover Township.
On the 8th of this month, by the Rev. F. W. Kremer, Mr. George U. Weir, with Miss Mary Gerret, both of this city [Lebanon].

Der Libanon Demokrat                           Lebanon, Pa.

January 16, 1852 Continued

On the 6th of this month, by the Rev. J. F. Messick, Mr. William R. Wilson, of Lancaster, with Miss Caroline Oberly, of Heidelberg Township, Lebanon County.
On the 23rd of December, by the Rev. C. A. Hay, Mr. Luther Fischer, with Miss Matilda M. Peiffer, of Palmyra.
On the 25th of December, by the Rev. A. Romich, Mr. Joseph G. Light, of Bethel Township, with Miss Rebecca Stroman, of North Annville Township.
On the 4th of this month, by the same [Rev. Romich], Mr. Heinrich Brough, with Miss Rebecca Schuger, both of North Annville Township.

January 23, 1852

Married. On the 17th of this month, by the Rev. Hand, Mr. Samuel M'Kinney, with Miss Sarah Ann Temple, both of Lebanon.
On the 15th of this month, by the Rev. G. F. Krotel, Mr. Jacob Becker, with Miss Elisabeth Gassert, both of South Lebanon Township.
On the 5th of this month, by Peter Stauch, Esq., Mr. Emanuel Eisenhauer, with Miss Caroline Hixenheiser, both of South Lebanon.
On the 10th, by the same [Peter Stauch], Mr. Henry Conner, with Miss Rebecca M'Kinny, both of South Lebanon Township.
[By the Rev. Mr. J. Stein.]
On the 10th of this month, Mr. Wilhelm Stub, of Upper Tulpehocken Township, Berks County, with Miss Rebecca Bergner, of Pinegrove Township, Schuylkill County.
On the 15th of this month, Mr. Johannes Batdorf, with Miss Anna Elisabeth Thompson, both of Swatara Township, Lebanon County.
On the 18th of this month, Mr. George Huntzinger, of Bethel Township, with Miss Catharina Yeagley, of Swatara Township.

January 30, 1852

Married. On the 27th of this month, by the Rev. G. F. Krotel, Mr. Jonathan Miller, of South Annville Township, with Miss Susannah Felty, of Swatara Township.
On the 22nd of this month, by the Rev. F. W. Kremer, Mr. William Umberger, of North Lebanon, with Miss Elisabeth Schneider, of South Lebanon Township.

February 6, 1852

Married. On the 3rd of February, by the Rev. H. Schrop,

Der Libanon Demokrat					Lebanon, Pa.

February 6, 1852 Continued

Mr. Jacob Peffly, with Miss Barbara Bliem, both of Swatara Township.
On the 22nd of January, by the Rev. J. Stein, Mr. Elias T. Gerberich, of Hanover, with Miss Susanna Schucker, of Bethel.
On the 24th, by the same [Rev. Stein], Mr. Isaac Rittel, of Bethel, with Miss Maria Schneider, of Jackson Township.
On the 6th of January, Mr. Jacob Graybill, with Miss Margaret Earley, of West Hanover, Dauphin County.
On the 25th, Mr. Cyrus Noll, of Bethel, with Miss Angelina Segner, of Palmyra.

February 13, 1852

Married. [By the Rev. Mr. A. Romig.]
On the 12th of January, Mr. Friederich Sporman, with Miss Regina Wennerich, both of Pinegrove, Schuylkill County.
On the 21st of January, Mr. Thomas Kreiser, of Union Township, with Miss Elisabeth Christ, of East Hanover Township.
[By the Rev. T. H. Leinbach.]
On the 18th of January, Mr. Jacob Albert, of Bethel Township, with Miss Catharina Phillippi, of Heidelberg Township.
On the 5th of this month, Mr. Samuel Aachenderfer, with Mary Schaffer, both of Lebanon County.
On the 5th of this month, by the Rev. G. F. Krotel, Mr. Joseph Steckbeck, of North Lebanon, with Miss Elisabeth Yeagley, of Swatara Township.
On the 29th of January, by the Rev. G. Van Nieda, Mr. Henry G. Wagner, of Tulpehocken, Berks County, with Miss Fianna Kelchner, of Jackson Township.

February 20, 1852

Married. On the 22nd of January, by the Rev. C. Siegrist, Mr. Daniel Weiss, of Lancaster County, with Miss Sarah Liveringshaus, of South Lebanon Townshp.
On the 17th of this month, by the Rev. G. F. Krotel, Mr. George Jury, of Campbelltown, with Miss Catharina Noll, of North Annville Township.
On the 16th of this month, by the Rev. Mr. Meyers, Mr. Walter Clark, of Millerstown, with Mrs. Leah Zimmerman, of this city.

February 27, 1852

Married. On Thursday, the 19th of this month, by the

Der Libanon Demokrat                           Lebanon, Pa.

February 27, 1852 Continued

Rev. Mr. Hartman, Mr. John Bender, of Londonderry Township, with Miss Catharina Silly, of Annville.
    On the 19th of this month, by the Rev. F. W. Kremer, Mr. Jacob Lehman, of Londonderry Township, with Miss Barbara Graby, of Lebanon County.
    On the 19th of this month, by the Rev. G. F. Krotel, Mr. Henry Witmer, with Miss Catharina Fies, both of South Lebanon.
    On the 22nd of this month, by the Rev. A. C. Wedekind, Mr. Henry Dohner, with Miss Harriet Royer, both of South Lebanon Township.

March 5, 1852

Married. On the 15th of February, by the Rev. C. Siegrist, Mr. Isaac Eberly, with Miss Julianna Evens, both of Heidelberg Township.
    On the 26th of February, by the Rev. T. H. Leinbach, Mr. Edward Witmyer, of South Lebanon, with Miss Maria Schimp, from the neighborhood of Womelsdorf, Berks County.
    On the day named [February 26], by the same [Rev. T. H. Leinbach], Mr. Jacob Ziebach, with Miss Lucetta Moyer, both of Bethel Township, Berks County.
    On the 26th of February, by the Rev. Mr. Schrop, Mr. Joseph Dohner, with Miss Maria Anna Rauch, both of South Lebanon.
    On the 17th of February, by J. B. Erb, Esq., Mr. Cyrus Binner, of Lebanon County, with Miss Susanna Carpenter, of Elisabeth Township, Lancaster County.
    On the 25th, by the Rev. Mr. Hand, Mr. John Fornwalt, with Miss Eleanor Youtz, both of Cornwall.

March 12, 1852

Married. On the 4th of this month, by the Rev. Mr. Romig, Mr. Moses Arndt, of Jonestown, with Miss Maria Reiser, of Marion Township, Berks County.

March 19, 1852

Married. On the 11th of this month, by the Rev. Mr. Wedekind, Mr. George Adams, of North Lebanon, with Miss Catharina A. Schneider, of Dauphin County.
    On the 6th of this month, by the Rev. Mr. Krotel, Mr. George Leininger, with Miss Elisabeth Schwartz, both of Swatara.
    On the 4th of this month, by the Rev. J. A. Sand, John Arndt, of Annville, with Miss Jane Stevenson, of Heidelberg.

Der Libanon Demokrat                    Lebanon, Pa.

### March 26, 1852

Married. On the 16th of this month, by the Rev. Mr. Romig, Mr. Joseph Herbst, with Miss Henriette Rank, both of East Hanover.
On the 21st of this month, by the Rev. Mr. Krotel, Peter Batdorf, with Angeline German, both of Jackson Township.
On the 18th of this month, by the same, Mr. G. W. Goodman, of East Hanover, Dauphin County, with Miss Leah Kretzmoyer, of Derry Township.
On the day named [March 18], by the same [ Rev. Krotel ], Mr. John Claus, with Susanna Reinoehl, both of Lebanon.
On the 18th of this month, John Donley, with Susanna Biener, both of Cornwall.
On the 18th of this month, by the Rev. A. C. Wedekind, Israel Gruber, with Elisabeth Henning, both of North Annville.
On the day named [March 18], by the same [Rev. A. C. Wedekind], Mr. Abraham Moyer, with Elisabeth Meiley, of East Hanover.

### April 2, 1852

Married. On the 24th of March, at Gettysburg, Rev. William D. Rodel, formerly of this city, with Miss Josephine Forney, of Gettysburg.

### April 9, 1852

Married. On the 25th of March, by the Rev. Mr. Meyer, Mr. Jacob Bender, of Annville, with widow Louisa Brunner, of Schwam, Lancaster County.
On the 31st of March, by the Rev. A. Romig, Mr. Henry Stager, with Miss Maria Rebock, both of East Hanover.
On the 1st of this month, by the Rev. W. W. Orwig, Mr. John Young, the young publisher of the 'Libanon Demokrat,' with Miss Elisabeth Rohland, of Union County.

### April 16, 1852

Married. On the 13th of this month, by the Rev. Mr. Kremer, Mr. John Long, with Miss Maria Lautenschlager, both of South Annville.
Some time ago, by the Rev. Mr. Thomas Leinbach, Mr. Cyrus Forrer, of Lebanon County, with Miss Leventine Zerbe, both of Tulpehocken, Berks County.
On the 3rd of this month, by the same [Rev. Thomas Leinbach], Mr. Jacob Giesey, with Miss Hannah Koch. Likewise Mr. Adam Wummer, with Miss Mary Ann Moyer, both of Bethel Township.

Der Libanon Demokrat                              Lebanon, Pa.

## April 16, 1852 Continued

Married. On the 10th of this month, by the same [Rev. Thomas Leinbach], Mr. Jonathan Schott, with Miss Mary Moyer, both of Bethel Township.

On the 11th, by the same [Rev. Thomas Leinbach], Mr. Peter Moyer, with Miss Sarah Daub, both of Jackson Township.

On the 4th of this month, by the Rev. Mr. Romich, Mr. Samuel Harnish, of Jackson Township, with Miss Retesa Pedre, of Bethel.

## April 23, 1852

On the 28th of March, by the Rev. Mr. Eckert, Jacob Rip, widower, with Miss Eva Hergleroth, both of Londonderry Township.

On the 10th of this month, by the Rev. D. Ulrich, Mr. John Gruber, of Heidelberg Township, Berks County, with Miss Elmira Schmalz, of Jackson Township, Lebanon County.

On the 11th of this month, by the Rev. D. Hertz, Mr. Henry B. Fetter, of Hinkeltown, with Miss Susannah Williams, of Lebanon County.

On the 11th of this month, by the Rev. F. W. Kremer, Mr. Samuel E. Mellinger, of Burlington, Iowa, with Miss Emeline A., 2nd daughter of the late Dr. John G. Marschall of Annville.

## May 21, 1852

Married. On the 12th of this month, in Reading, Josiah Funk, Esq., of this city [Lebanon], with Miss Bell Marschall of Reading.

On the 13th of this month, by the Rev. F. W. Kremer, Mr. William Miller, with Miss Eliza Oswald, both of this city [Lebanon].

On the same day [May 13], by the same [Rev. F. W. Kremer], Mr. Jacob Noll, with Miss Catharina Ingrum, of North Lebanon.

## May 28, 1852

Married. On the 25th of this month, by the Rev. G. F. Krotel, Mr. Edward D. Ives, of Berks County, with Miss Mary Ann Stager, of Lebanon.

On the 23rd of this month, by the Rev. Mr. Oram, Mr. George Schay, with Miss Louisa Seltzer, both of this city.

Sometime ago, Mr. Andrew Teiss, formerly of Lebanon, with Miss Maria Eckel, of Tremont, Schuylkill County.

Der Libanon Demokrat　　　　　　　　　　Lebanon, Pa.

## May 28, 1852 Continued

Married. On the 18th of this month, by the Rev. Ziegenfuss, Mr. Elijah Walborn, with Miss Elisa Maulfair, both of North Annville.

On the 20th of this month, by the same [Rev. Ziegenfuss], Mr. Israel Light, with Miss Rosanna Kochenderfer, both of Lebanon.

## June 11, 1852

Married. On the 25th of May, by the Rev. Mr. Stein, Mr. Heinrich Kemmerer, with Miss Rosanna Miller, both of Hanover, Lebanon County.

On the 20th of May, by the same [Rev. Stein], Samuel Boeshore, with Miss Maria Weiss, both of Union Township, Lebanon County.

On the day named [May 20], by the same [Rev. Stein], Mr. David Uhrig, of Bethel Township, with Anna Christ, of Jackson Township.

On the 3rd of June, by the same [Rev. Stein[, Jacob High, with Miss Maria Kuhns, both of Union Township.

Some time ago, by the same [Rev. Stein], Mr. _____ Behny, with Sarah Weiss, both of Union Township, Lebanon County.

On the 27th of May, by the Rev. A. Romich, Mr. Wilhelm Yingst, with Miss Maria Anna Brauch, both of Annville Township, Lebanon County.

On the 30th of May, by the same, Mr. Adam Schaly, of Swatara, with Miss Maria Brand, of North Lebanon Township.

On the 3rd of this month, by the Rev. G. F. Krotel, Mr. John Gasser, with Miss Elian Schmidt, both of South Lebanon Township.

On the day named [June 3], by the same [Rev. Krotel], Mr. John Lantz, of South Lebanon Township, with Miss Eliza Bender, of Lebanon

On the 3rd of this month, by the Rev. F. W. Kremer, Mr. John F. Peck, of Dauphin County, with Miss Ann Juline Stober, of Heidelberg Township, Lebanon County.

## June 18, 1852

Married. On the 1st of this month, by the Rev. Mr. Eggers, Mr. Levi Werner, with Miss Maria Eschelberger, both of Jackson Township.

On the day named [June 1], by the Rev. Mr. Pauli, Mr. David C. Keller, of Union Deposit, Dauphin County, with Miss Catharina B. Witmer, of Lebanon County.

On the 3rd of May, by the Rev. T. H. Leinbach, Mr. Levi Wolfersberger, of Tulpehocken, Berks County, with Miss Catharina Gruber, of South Annville Township.

Der Libanon Demokrat                           Lebanon, Pa.
                        June 25, 1852

Married. On the 3rd of this month, by the Rev. John T. Smith, Mr. John Meily of Jonestown, with Miss Helen L. Halter, of Washington City.
 On the 10th of June, in Myerstown, by the Rev. Mr. Van Nieda, Mr. David W. Spangler, of Elisabeth Township, Lancaster County, with Miss Elisabeth Mays, of Lebanon County.
 On the 22nd of June, by the Rev. Mr. Schrop, Mr. Johannes H. Keller, with Miss Sarah Richard, both of this county.
 By the Rev. Thomas H. Leinbach: some time ago, Mr. David Backholder, of Jackson, Lebanon County, with Miss Malinda Lebengood, of Tulpehocken, Berks County. - On the 4th of this month, Mr. John Walborn, of Bethel, Lebanon County, with Mrs. Catharina Moyer, of Bethel, Berks County.

                        July 2, 1852

Married. On the 22nd of June, by the Rev. G. F. Krotel, Mr. John Stoever, of North Lebanon Township, with Miss Elisabeth Bergelbach, of the city of Lebanon.

                        July 9, 1852

Married. On the 1st of this month, by the Rev. G. F. Krotel, Mr. William Bicher, of Lebanon, with Miss Louisa H. Embich, of Myerstown.
 On the 4th of this month, by the Rev. Mr. Kremer, Mr. Jacob W. Miller, with Miss Catharina Landis, both of Heidelberg Township, Lebanon County.

                        July 23, 1852

Married. On the 22nd of last June, by the Rev. J. Stein, Mr. Thomas Boeshor, with Miss Magdalena Schuey, both of Union Township.
 On the 4th of July, by the same [Rev. J. Stein], Mr. Josua Smitt, with Miss Lawina Fischer, both of North Annville Township.

                        July 30, 1852

Married. On the 22nd of this month, by the Rev. C. W. Hutter, Mr. Anthony S. Ely, with Miss Lizzie S. Goschert, both of this city.
 On the 27th of this month, by the Rev. Mr. Kremer, Mr. George Reinhard, with Miss Matilda Seltzer, both of this city.

Der Libanon Demokrat						Lebanon, Pa.

### July 30, 1852 Continued

Married. On the 25th of July, by the Rev. H. Schrop, Mr. Daniel Keller, of North Lebanon, with Miss Catharina Achenbach, of Berks County.

### August 6, 1852

Married. On the 29th of July, by the Rev. Mr. Oram, Mr. William H. Lascomb, with Miss Jane G. Knox, both of this city [Lebanon].
    On the 18th of July, by the Rev. A. Romich, Mr. Tobias R. Bender, of Union, with Miss Belinda Schade, of Swatara Township.
    On the 29th of June, by the same [Rev. A. Romich], Mr. Johann Martz, of North Lebanon, with Rebecca Wolf, of Bethel Township.

### August 13, 1852

Married. On the 5th of this month, by the Rev. G. Oram, Mr. Samuel Bell, of Baltimore, with Miss Rosanna Schank, of Cornwall, Lebanon County.

### August 20, 1852

Married. On the 8th of this month, by the Rev. John Gring, Mr. John Bixler, of Monroe Valley, Berks County, with Miss Subina Sattazan, formerly of Mt. Hope Furnace, Lebanon County.
    On the 12th of this month, in Reading, by the Rev. Mr. Richards, Charles Brotherlein, of Lebanon, with Miss Sarah H., daughter of Sam'l Hauck, of South Lebanon.
    On the 22nd of July, by the Rev. C. A. Hay, Mr. Reuben Bischop, with Miss Elisabeth Killinger, both of Palmyra.
    On the 15th of this month, by the Rev. John Moyer, Mr. William Richardson, with Miss Elisabeth Schnurly, both of Elisabeth Township, Lancaster County.

### September 3, 1852

Married. On the 27th of this month, by the Rev. Mr. Ditzler, Mr. Michael Alleman, of Dauphin County, with Miss Leah Royer, of Heidelberg.
    On the 24th of August, by the Rev. T. H. Leinbach, Mr. Henry Spengler, of Jackson, with Miss Catharina Yingst of Heidelberg.
    On the 26th, by the Rev. Mr. Kremer, Mr. Cyrus Bemerderfer, with Miss Catharina Gerhart, both of North Lebanon.

Der Libanon Demokrat                    Lebanon, Pa.

                September 10, 1852

Married. On the 31st of August, by Henry K. Boyer, Esq.,
Mr. Gordon R. Goff, with Mrs. Maria Reichelderfer, both
of the Union Water Works, Lebanon County.
    On the 7th of this month, by the Rev. H. Schrop,
Mr. Solomon Miller, with Miss Elisabeth Kreider, both
of East Hanover Township.
    On the 26th of August, by the Rev. Mr. Bollinger,
Mr. J. F. Wenger, of Swatara Township, with Miss Elisabeth Moyer, of Jackson Township.
    On the 2nd of this month, by the Rev. G. F. Krotel,
Mr. Johann Eisenman, with Miss Catharina Schiffer, both
of South Lebanon Township.

                September 17, 1852

Married. On the 6th of this month, by the Rev. Mr. Wedekind, Mr. J. G. Peleger, with Miss Elisabeth Carl, both
of the vicinity of Schaefferstown.
    On the 11th of this month, by the Rev. Mr. Krotel,
Mr. Martin Brandt, with Miss Rebecca Miller, both of
Annville, Lebanon County.
    On the 9th of this month, by the Rev. Mr. Kremer,
Mr. Jacob Kratzer, of Lebanon County, with Miss Esther
Berkheiser, of Lancaster County.

                September 24, 1852

Married. On last Tuesday [September 21], by the Rev.
Mr. Wedekind, Mr. John Wolf, with Miss Rosanna Licht,
both of this city [Lebanon].

                October 1, 1852

Married. On the 23rd of September by the Rev. G. F. Krotel, Mr. Tobias Reinohl, with Miss Catharina Eby, both
of this city [Lebanon].
    On the 23rd of September, by the Rev. G. F. Krotel,
Buschrod W. Hughes, of Schuylkill County, with Miss Sarah
Schindel, daughter of Mr. John Schindel, Esq., of this
city [Lebanon].
    On the 28th of September, in this city [Lebanon],
by the Rev. G. F. Krotel, Mr. Andrew H. Embich, with Miss
Jane A. Flory.
    On the 28th of September, by the Rev. A. C. Wedekind, Mr. Friedrich Koch, with Miss Mary Ann Brubaker,
both of Lancaster County.
    On the 23rd of September, by the Rev. F. W. Kremer,
Mr. Peter Schally, with Miss Amelia Licht [Light], both
of North Lebanon.
    On the 2nd of September, by Mr. Weinberg, Moritz Lob,

Der Libanon Demokrat                    Lebanon, Pa.

October 1, 1852 Continued

publisher of the Doylestown Morning Star, formerly of Lebanon, with Miss Emilie Lob, of Philadelphia.

October 8, 1852

Married. On the 26th of September, by the Rev. J. Kleinfelter, Mr. Samul Karra, of South Lebanon Township, with Miss Leah Clay, of Heidelberg Township.
On the 30th of September, by the Rev. G. F. Krotel, Mr. Henry Flagg, with Miss Ephia Long, both of South Annville.
On the day named [September 30], by the same [Rev. G. F. Krotel], Mr. John Lob, of Dauphin County, with Miss Elisabeth Killwell of Londonderry Township, Lebanon County.
On the day named [September 30], by the same [Rev. G. F. Krotel], Mr. John S. Heisy, of Lebanon County, with Miss Elisabeth McClemmings, of Dauphin County.
On the 30th of September, by the Rev. G. Oram, Mr. George Schay, of North Lebanon, with Miss Ann Baldwin, of Cornwall Furnace.

October 15, 1852

Married. On the 7th of this month, by the Rev. G. F. Krotel, Mr. Samuel Fies, with Susanna Hoffert, both of South Lebanon Township.
On the 30th of September, by the Rev. A. C. Wedekind, Mr. Henry S. Gerberich, of East Hanover, with Miss Mary Anna Glick, of Bethel Township.
On the 9th of this month, by the Rev. Chr. Siegrist, Mr. William Weiss, with Miss Mary Schram, both of Millcreek.
On the 7th of this month, by the Rev. Mr. Stein, Mr. John Bender, widower of South Annville, with Sarah Bolz, widower of North Annville Township.
On the 7th of this month, by the Rev. F. W. Kremer, Mr. George Bleistein of this city, with Miss Sarah Blecker, of this county.

December 10, 1852

Married. On the 5th of this month, by the Rev. Mr. Eggers, Mr. William Strickler, with Miss Elisabeth Breittigain, both of Millcreek Township.
On the 30th of November, by the Rev. Yeager, Mr. John Klick, with Miss Rebecca Wolf, both of Jackson Township.
On the 2nd of this month, by the Rev. F. W. Kremer, Mr. Henry Schenk, with Miss Margaret Schram, both of

Der Libanon Demokrat					Lebanon, Pa.

December 10, 1852 Continued

South Lebanon Township.
On the 7th of this month, by the Rev. Mr. Stein, Mr. George Eisenhauer, with Catharina Clemens, both of East Hanover.

December 17, 1852

Married. On the 9th of this month, by the Rev. Mr. Krotel, Mr. George Lantz, of South Lebanon, with Miss Malinda Dubs, of this city [Lebanon].
On the 30th of November, by the Rev. J. Stein, Mr. John Kohr, with Miss Catharina Pauer, both of Union Township.
On the 2nd of this month, by the same, Mr. Daniel Uhrich, of East Hanover Township, with Miss Rebecca Poorman, of West Hanover Township, Dauphin County.
On the 7th of this month, by the same [Rev. J. Stein], Mr. George Eisenhauer, with Miss Catharina Clemens, both of Hanover Township.
On the 5th of this month, by the Rev. Mr. Krotel, Mr. Henry Ebersole, of Lancaster County, with Miss Catharina Ebrecht, of Lebanon County.
On the 4th of this month, by the Rev. Mr. Gring, Mr. John Lesster, with Miss Sarah Daniel, both of Jackson Township.

January 7, 1853

Married. On the 11th of November, by the Rev. Mr. Gring, Mr. Simon Walmer, with Miss Rebecca Klein, both of Union Township.
On the 4th of December, by the same [Rev. Gring], Mr. Johannes Li__er with Sarah Daniel, both of Jackson Township, Lebanon County.
On the 28th of December, by the same [Rev. Gring], Mr. Frnklin Donmoyer, with Miss Adelina Scherdel, both of Union Township, Lebanon County.
On the 25th of December, Mr. Benneville Hummel, with Miss Louisa Zerver, both of Schuylkill County.
On the 19th of December, by the Rev. Mr. Stein, Mr. David Emrich, of North Lebanon, with Miss Elisabeth Noll of Bethel Township.
On the 23rd of December, by the same [Rev. Stein], Mr. Gernelius Fuchs, of Dauphin County, with Maria Federulf, of East Hanover, Lebanon County.
On the day named [December 23], by the same [Rev. Stein], Mr. William Schul of Swatara, with Miss Carolina Stein, of Union Township, Lebanon County.
On the 23rd of this month, by the Rev. Jonathan E. Hiester, Dr. Henry Fahnestock, of North Annville, with

43

Der Libanon Demokrat                           Lebanon, Pa.

January 7, 1853 Continued

Miss Sarah Ann Carper, of South Annville.
On the same day [December 23], by the same [Rev. Jonathan E. Hiester], Mr. Daniel Wagner, of Londonderry, with Miss Marie Yingst likewise of Londonderry.
On the 30th of December, by the same [Rev. Jonathan E. Hiester], Mr. Henry Smith of North Annville, with Miss Elisabeth Boyer, of South Annville.
On the 23rd of December, Mr. Henry B. Seidel, of the Monroe Iron Works, near Fredericksburg, with Miss Emma G. Brandt, of Pinegrove, Schuylkill County.
On the 30th of December, by the Rev. G. F. Krotel, Mr. Abraham Dutter, of East Hanover Township, with Miss Sarah Karmeny, of North Lebanon.

January 14, 1853

Married. On the 6th of this month, by the Rev. G. F. Krotel, Mr. Aaron Fox, with Miss Carolina Fischer, both of North Lebanon.
On the 14th of November, by Joseph Henry Esq., Mr. Samuel Buchter of East Hanover, with Miss Sarah Yingst, of North Annville.
On the 4th of this month, by the Rev. W. L. Reber, Mr. Isaac Noll, of Newmanstown, with Miss Polly Dengler, of Schaefferstown, Lebanon County.
On the 4th of this month, by the Rev. G. F. Krotel, Mr. Jacob K. Francis, of Berks County, with Miss Eliada E. Breitenbach, of Myerstown, Lebanon County.

January 21, 1853

Married. On the 7th of this month, by the Rev. Laitzle, Mr. Edward Dissinger, with Miss Elisabeth Rotharmel, both of Campbelltown.
On the 13th of this month, by the same, Mr. Samuel Detweiler, of Harrisburg, with Miss Elisabeth Matter of Palmyra.
On the 13th of this month, by the Rev. Mr. Kremer, Mr. John Haak, with Miss Elisabeth Fitterer, both of South Lebanon Township.
On the 23rd of December, by the Rev. D. Ulrich, Mr. Jacob Bricker, of Newmanstown, with Miss Elisabeth Ann Gruber, of Marion Township.

January 28, 1853

Married, On the 13th of this month, by the Rev. Mr. Kremer, Mr. John Haak, with Miss Elisabeth Fitterer, both of South Lebanon Township
On the 16th of January, by the Rev. J. Stein, Mr.

Der Libanon Demokrat                    Lebanon, Pa.

January 28, 1853 Continued

Henry Derkes, with Miss Elisabeth Hess, both of Bethel Township.
On the 18th of January, by the same [Rev. Stein], Mr. William Gembel, with Miss Magdalena Wagner, both of Bethel Township.
On the 20th of January, by the same [Rev. Stein], Mr. Elias Gerberich, of East Hanover Township, with Miss Lydia Philips, of Bethel Township.

February 11, 1853

Married. On the 27th of January, by the Rev. Mr. Daniel Hertz, Mr. Henry Mischler, merchant of Reading, with Miss Diana Kahlbach, of Lebanon County.
On the 3rd of this month, by the Rev. F. W. Kremer, Mr. Elias Yordy, of South Annville, with Miss Anna M., daughter of Daniel Fegan, Sheriff of Lebanon County.

February 18, 1853

Married. On the 27th of January, by the Rev. John Stein, Mr. John Henry Bross, of Ohio, with Miss Amanda Boeshore, of Swatara Township.
On the 3rd of February, by the same [Rev. Stein], Mr. Tobias Loos, of Bethel Township, with Miss Maria Ritter, of North Lebanon Township.
On the 10th of February, by the same [Rev. Stein], Mr. Adam Hemperly, of Londonderry Township, with Miss Rebecca Scheppler, of Swatara Township.
On the 6th of this month, by the Rev. William G. Laitzel, Mr. John B. Wieland, of Elizabethtown, Lancaster County, with Elisabeth Wolfersberger, of Campbelltown.
On the 15th of this month, by the Rev. Mr. Laitzle, Mr. Michael Spayd, of Hummelstown, with Miss Maria Ann Garber, of Palmyra.
On the 13th of this month, by the Rev. G. F. Krotel, Mr. George McLaughlin, of North Lebanon, with Miss Elisabeth Ely of Schaefferstown.

February 25, 1853

Married. On the 3rd of February, by the Rev. George Schmidt, Mr. Isaac Ried, with Miss Hannah Achenbach, both of South Annville Township.
On the day named [February 3], by the same [Rev. George Schmidt], Mr. Cornelius Schmidt, with Miss Carolina Bar, both of North Annville Township.

Der Libanon Demokrat                    Lebanon, Pa.

## March 4, 1853

Married. On the 20th of February, by the Rev. John Gring, Mr. Edward Heffelfinger, formerly of Myerstown, with Miss Sarah Wagner of Fredericksburg.

On the day named [February 20], by the Rev. G. F. Krotel, Mr. George Henry Hartman, with Miss Anna Maria Bender, of Lancaster.

On the 21st of February, by the Rev. Christian Siegrist, Mr. Henry Riehm, with Miss Anna Scharp, both of Heidelberg Township.

On the 15th of February, by Mr. John Stein, Mr. John Rauch, of Bethel Township, Berks County, with Miss Magdalena Gerberich, of East Hanover Township, Lebanon County.

On the 17th of February, by the same [Rev. Stein], Mr. Israel Rieth, with Miss Elisabeth Heilman, both of North Annville Township.

## March 11, 1853

Married. On the 1st of March, by the Rev. J. M. Dieter, Mr. John Krall, of Hanover, with Miss Sarah Phillippi, of Schaefferstown.

On the 6th of this month, by the Rev. Mr. Krotel, William Uhrich, with Miss Rebecca Hammer, both of this city [Lebanon].

## March 18, 1853

Married. On the 11th of this month, by the Rev. John Stein, Mr. Samuel Lang, of Jonestown, with Miss Longenecker, of Dauphin County.

On the 17th of February, by the Rev. Mr. Laitzle, Mr. Abraham Madder, of Unie (?), with Miss Catharina Walmer, of Dauphin County.

On the 24th, by the same [Rev. Laitzle], Mr. William Schertzer, with Miss Elisabeth Black, both of Annville.

On the 15th of this month, by the Rev. Mr. Leinbach, Mr. Christopher Carmany, of Londonderry, with widow Diehl, of Myerstown.

On the 17th of this month, by the Rev. Mr. Kremer, Mr. Henry Smith, with Miss Amanda Henning, both of this city [Lebanon].

## March 25, 1853

Married. On the 17th of March, by the Rev. Mr. Schrop, Mr. Joseph Klein, widower of Union Township, with Sarah Peffley, widow of Swatara Township.

Der Libanon Demokrat                    Lebanon, Pa.

March 25, 1853 Continued

Married. On the 20th of March, by the same [Rev. Schrop], Mr. Andreas Ross, with Miss Rosanna Blouch, both of North Lebanon.
On the 20th of this month, by the Rev. Mr. Wedekind, Henry Cox, with Barbara Bauman, both of South Lebanon.
On the 22nd, by the same [Rev. Wedekind], Mr. W. G. Ward, of North Lebanon, with Miss Mary Ann Strickler, of this city [Lebanon].

April 1, 1853

Married. On the 27th of March, by the Rev. G. F. Krotel, Mr. Peter Nagel_oner, of Reading, with Miss Mary Ann Ziegler, of Myerstown.
On the 13th of March, by the Rev. Thomas Yeager, Mr. John B. Quimbe, of Boston, Mass., with Miss Agnes H. Stephen, of Womerlsodrf, Berks County.

April 8, 1853

Married. On the 26th of March, by the Rev. Thomas Yeager, Mr. John Ritschert, of Berks County, with Mrs. Eva Ritschert, of Millcreek Township, Lebanon County.
On the 29th of March, by the Rev. John Stein, Mr. Carl Rosenberger, of Hummelstown, Dauphin County, with Miss Sarah Bender, of East Hanover Township.

April 22, 1853

Married. On the 14th of this month, by the Rev. George Schmidt, Mr. Johann Pannebecker, of Palmyra, with Miss Maria Miller, os South Annville Township.
On the 14th of this month, by the Rev. G. F. Krotel, Mr. John Braun, of East Hanover Township, with Miss Catharina Scherk, of North Lebanon Township.

April 29, 1853

Married. On the 26th of this month, by the Rev. Mr. Romig, Mr. Henry D. Bieber, of Annville, with Miss Rosanna Cooper, of Mt. Nebo, Lebanon County.
On the 17th of April, by the Rev. H. Schrop, Mr. Henry Miller, of Fredericksburg, with Miss Nancy Blauch, of North Lebanon.

May 6, 1853

Married. On the 19th of April, by the Rev. Yeager, Mr. John Leininger, of Womelsdorf, with Miss Rebecca Numan

Der Libanon Demokrat					Lebanon, Pa.

### May 6, 1853 Continued

[Newman], of Lebanon County.
    On the 16th, by the same [Rev. Yeager], Mr. John Ingham, with Miss Frances Hackman, both of Myerstown.
    On the 28th of April, by the Rev. George Schmidt, Mr. Moses Boyer, of Jonestown, with Miss Mary Wendling of Union Township.
    On the 15th, in Philadelphia, by the Rev. Grunbank, Mr. Jackson O'Brien, with Miss Anna Barbara Scott, formerly of this city [Lebanon].

### May 13, 1853

Married. On the 28th of April, by the Rev. William G. Laitzle, Mr. John Albert, with Miss Mary Ann Quigley, both of Londonderry.
    On the 20th, by the same [Rev. William G. Laitzle], Mr. Samuel Killinger, of Franklin County, with Margaret Killinger, of Londonderry Township.
    On the 11th of this month, by the Rev. Harbach, Mr. Cyrus Hamilton, of Lebanon, with Miss Henrietta Kaufman, of the city of Lancaster.
    On the 24th of May, by the Rev. Mr. Groller, Mr. Philip Schaffer, of Dauphin County, with Miss Elisabeth Seybert, of East Hanover, Lebanon County. [It seems the printer may have erred in setting the type for this marriage. Most likely the date was April 24.]

### May 20, 1853

Married by the Rev. John Stein.
    On the 30th of last April, Mr. Daniel Spankuch [Spancake], with Miss Susanna Schmidt, both of Bethel Township, Lebanon County.
    On the 7th instant of May, Mr. Isaac Smith, with Miss Caroline Rudy, both of the aforesaid township and county.
    On the 8th, Mr. Levi Umberger, of Swatara Township, Lebanon County, with Miss Elisabeth Ochsenreiter [Oxenreider], of Bethel Township, Berks County.

### May 27, 1853

Married. On the 15th of May, by the Rev. John Stein, Mr. Jeremiah Karmeny, of Annville Township, with Miss Carolina Batdorf, of Jackson Township.
    On the 16th of May, by the same [Rev. John Stein], Mr. William Kern, of Richland County, Ohio, with Miss Catharina Satazahn, of Swatara Township.
    On the 17th of May, by the same [Rev. Stein], Mr. Johannes Herschberger, with Miss Hannah Naftzinger, both

Der Libanon Demokrat                          Lebanon, Pa.

              May 27, 1853 Continued

of Union Township.
    On the 19th of May, by the same [Rev. Stein], Mr.
Jacob Deck, of Marion Township, Berks County, with widow
Maria Albert, of East Hanover Township.

                  June 3, 1853

Married. On the 17th of May, by the Rev. T. H. Leinbach,
Mr. Herman Wolf, with Miss Magdalena Schaffer, both of
Lebanon County.
    On the 28th of April, by the Rev. G. L. Eggers, Mr.
Levi Lehman, with Miss Mary Cox, both of Myerstown.
    On the 15th of May, by the Rev. A. S. Leinbach, Mr.
Philip Gelsinger, of West Cocalico Township, Lancaster
County, with Miss Sara Weik, of Millcreek Township, Leb-
anon County.

                  June 10, 1853

Married. On the 2nd of this month, by the Rev. August
C. Wedekind, John W. Ulrich, Esq., with Miss Mary A. Bau-
man, both of this city [Lebanon].
    On the 31st of May, by the Rev. Mr. J. E. Hiester,
Mr. Joseph H. Matz, of Schuylkill County, with Miss Maria
E. Ulrich, of North Annville, Lebanon County.
    On the 2nd of this month, by the Rev. Mr. Laitzle,
Mr. David Craiglow, of Palmyra, with Miss Rebecca Stroh,
of Annville.

                  June 24, 1853

Married. On the 16th of June, by the Rev. A. Romich,
Mr. Peter Reth, with Miss Lidia Krupp, both of Lebanon
County.

                  July 1, 1853

Married. On the 15th of June, by the Rev. P. B. Mauger,
Mr. R. Hean, with Miss Lucetta Ritschert, both of Belle-
view [Bellegrove].
    On the 16th of June, by the Rev. J. E. Hiester, Mr.
George Segner, of Palmyra, with Miss Emma Schauers, of
Annville.
    On the 29th of May, by the Rev. Mr. Stein, Mr. Levi
Hauer, with Miss Catharina Braun, both of Bethel Town-
ship, Lebanon County.
    On the 14th of June, by the same, Mr. Adam Licht
[Light], with Miss Frenica Ober, both of North Annville
Township.

Der Libanon Demokrat                              Lebanon, Pa.
               July 1, 1853 Continued

Married. On the 19th of June, by the same [Rev. Stein],
Mr. Johannes Sattezahn, of Swatara Township, with widow
Amanda Weiss, of Hanover.

                    July 8, 1853

Married. On the 19th of June, by the Rev. William G.
Laitzel, Mr. John Kiefer, with Miss Rosa Killinger, both
of Londonderry Township.
     On the 3rd of July, by the Rev. John Kleinfelter,
Mr. William Bechtel, with Miss Catharina Frankhauser,
both of West Cocalico Township, Lancaster County.
     On the 3rd of this month, by the Rev. Christian
Siegrist, Mr. Michael Noll, with Miss Caroline Bell,
both of Heidelberg Township.
     On the day named [June 3], by the same [Rev. Christ-
ian Siegrist], Mr. Elias Eberly, with Miss Sarah Fessler,
both of Heidelberg Township.
     On the 16th of June, by the Rev. Mr. Carper, Mr.
Joseph Beeber, with Miss Sarah Miller, both of Pinegrove,
Schuylkill County.

                    July 15, 1853

Married. On the 30th of June, by the Rev. Theo T. Yeager,
Mr. Joseph Schantz, with Miss Purmilla Derr, both of the
city of Lebanon.
     On the 30th of June, by the Rev. A. B. Casper, Mr.
John G. Fuss, formerly of Myerstown, with Miss Lydia
Schwartzenner, of New Berlin, Union County.
     By the Rev. Mr. Gring:
     On the 21st of last May, Mr. Elias Wagner, with Miss
Sarah Gerloff, both of Jackson Township.
     On the 28th of May, Mr. Schreckengast, with Miss Re-
becca Guth, both of Union Township.
     On the 3rd of this month, Mr. George Brossman, of
Bethel Township, with Miss Jane Buchmoyer, of Fredericks-
burg, Lebanon County.
     On the day named [July 3], Mr. Joseph Eisenhauer,
with Miss Maria Anna Ditzler, both of Fredericksburg.

                    July 22, 1853

Married. On the 10th of this month, by the Rev. Mr.
Siegrist, Mr. Josuah Yocum, with Miss Polly Strickler,
both of Schaefferstown.
     On the 17th of July, by the Rev. Mr. Schrop, Mr.
Abraham Peffly, of Swatara Township, with Miss Nancy Miller, of North Annville.

Der Libanon Demokrat                    Lebanon, Pa.

July 29, 1853

Married. On the 10th of this month, by the Rev. Tho. T. Yeager, Mr. John Batdorf, of Jackson Township, with Miss Susanna Beckley, of Myerstown.

August 12, 1853

Married. On the 2nd of August, by the Rev. Mr. Sarper, Mr. Jacob Muschler of Kiprerheim, with Miss Elisabetha Bauman, of Smithheim, both of _____ _____ and now residing in Seltzersville, Lebanon County.

August 19, 1853

Married. On the 28th of July, by the Rev. J. Stein, Mr. George Redford, with Miss Maria Sched, both of Union Township.
On the 11th of August, by the same [Rev. J. Stein], Mr. John Tittel, with Miss Lovina Riehm, both of West Hanover, Dauphin County.
On the 11th of this month, by the Rev. F. W. Kremer, Mr. Henry H. Snavely, with Miss Lydia Ann Bretz, both of North Lebanon.
On the 9th of this month, by the Rev. Mr. Siegrist, Mr. Edward Fetter, of Elisabeth Township, Lancaster County, with Miss Anna Matthews, of Heidelberg Township, Lebanon County.

August 26, 1853

Married. By the Rev. Thomas H. Leinbach.
On the 2nd of this month, Mr. Isaac Bechtel, with Miss Elisabeth Weber, both of Millersburg, Berks County.
On the 7th of this month, Mr. Jonathan Forrer, with Miss Mary Hartman, all of Berks County.
On the 21st of this month, Mr. Jeremias Achey, of Heidelberg Township, Lebanon County, with Miss Susanna Ruth, of Cocalico Township, Lancaster County.
On the day named [August 21], Mr. John Achey, of Heidelberg Township, Lebanon County, with Miss Louise Walter, of Lancaster County.
On the 11th of this month, by the Rev. William G. Laitzle, Mr. Peter Yingst, with Miss Lydia Wengert, both of Dauphin County.
On the 18th of August, by the Rev. J. E. Hiester, Mr. John Peter, with Miss Carolina Miller, both of Annville, Lebanon County.

September 2, 1853

Married. On the 10th of last July, by the Rev. A. Romich,

Der Libanon Demokrat						Lebanon, Pa.

### September 2, 1853 Continued

Mr. Joseph B. Bates, with Miss Lewina Jennings, both of East Hanover Township.
    On the 7th of August, by the same minister [Rev. A. Romich], Mr. John M'Gee, with Miss Elisabeth Kercher, both of Monroe Valley.
    On the 21st of August, by the same minister [Rev. A. Romich], Mr. Henry Heilman, with Miss Drusilla Spittler, both of Jonestown.
    On the 25th of August, by the Rev. F. W. Kremer, Mr. Jacob Reckenberger, with Miss Rebecca Blauch, both of North Annville.
    On the 23rd of August, by the Rev. Mr. Hertz, Mr. Jonas Stohr, of Ashland County, Ohio, with Miss Sarah Enck, of New Ephrata, Lancaster County.
    On the 30th of August, by the Rev. Mr. Eggers, William Uhrich, Esq., of Myerstown, with Miss Sarah Magdalena, daughter of the Rev. T. H. Leinbach, of Tulpehocken, both of Lebanon County.

### September 9, 1853

Married. On the 1st of this month, by the Rev. Mr. Zug, Mr. Henry, son of John Herschey, with Miss Barbara, daughter of John Longenecker, of Conewago, both of Dauphin County.
    On the 13th of this month, by the Rev. Ulrich, Jonathan Reinoehl, of Jackson Township, with Miss Rosina Barton, of Marion Township, Berks County.

### September 16, 1853

Married. On the 16th of this month, by the Rev. Mr. Wedekind, Mr. William Moore, with Miss Elisabeth Schindel, both of this city [Lebanon].

### September 23, 1853

Married. On the 19th of this month, by the Rev. J. E. Hiester, Mr. John Bard, with Miss Margaret Darkes, both of Annville, Lebanon County.

### September 30, 1853

Married. On the 26th of this month, by the Rev. Mr. Hiester, Mr. William Ault, of North Annville, with Miss Mary Ann Reissner, of North Lebanon.
    On the 19th of this month, by the same [Rev. Hiester], Mr. John Ward, with Miss Margaret Darkes, both of Annville.
    On the 4th of this month, by the Rev. Mr. Stein, Mr. William Loser, with Elisabeth Sattezahn, both of Swatara.

Der Libanon Demokrat                    Lebanon, Pa.

            September 30, 1853 Continued

Married. On the 14th of this month, by the same [Rev. Stein], David Kleimer, with Elisabeth Behny, both of Swatara.

                October 7, 1853

Married. On the 4th of this month, by the Rev. Wedekind, Mr. Isaac Reber, with Miss Lovina Hawk, both of Myerstown.
      On the 29th of September, by the same [Rev. Wedekind], Mr. Felix B. Light, of South Lebanon, with Miss Catharina Wittenmeyer, of South Annville.
      On the 27th, by the Rev. Kremer, Mr. John Brandt, with Miss Susan Dubbs, both of this city [Lebanon].

                October 14, 1853

Married. On the 29th of September, by the Rev. Thomas H. Leinbach, Mr. Cyrus Yingst, of Jackson Township, with Lodia Boyer, of North Annville Township.
      On the day named [September 29], by the same [Rev. Thomas H. Leinbach], Mr. Solomon Schwob, of North Lebanon, with Susanna Gerhart, of Cocalico Township, Lancaster County.

                October 21, 1853

Married. By the Rev. D. Ulrich: On the 8th of this month, Mr. George N. Moyer, with Amanda Petree, both of Womelsdorf.
      By the Rev. J. M. Ditzler, of Stouchsburg: on the 6th of this month, Benjamin Auman, with Mary Ann Becky, both of Upper Tulpehocken, Berks County. - on the 13th, William Fasnacht with Elisabeth Zeller, both of Jackson, Lebanon County. - Carl Zimmerman of Upper Tulpehocken, Berks County, with Catharina Maurer of Jackson Township, Lebanon County.

                October 28, 1853

Married. On the 25th of this month, by the Rev. Mr. Yeager, Mr. Isaac S. Gerhard, of West Cocalico, Lancaster County, with Sarah Ann Spohn, of Spring Township, Berks County.
      By the Rev. Mr. Stein.
      On the 6th of October, Mr. John Deck, of Bethel Township, Berks County, with Miss Susanna Groff, of Bethel Township, Lebanon County.
      On the day named [October 6], Mr. Henry Houtz, with Sarah Gundrum, both of Bethel Township, Lebanon County.

                     53

Der Libanon Demokrat                           Lebanon, Pa.
              October 28, 1853 Continued

Married. On the 20th of October, David Killinger with Elisabeth Ramler, both of Hanover Township, Dauphin County.
   On the 15th of October, David Fieman, with Lodia Gehret, both of Bethel Township, Lebanon County.

                  November 4, 1853
Married. By the Rev. Thomas H. Leinbach.
   On the 13th of October, Mr. William Wilhelm, of Marion, with Miss Leventina Schneider, of Bethel, both of Berks County.
   On the 22nd, Mr. David Palm, with Miss Elisabeth Mutschler, both of North Heidelberg, Berks County.
   On the 23rd, Mr. Henry Giesey, of North Lebanon, with Miss Sarah Dissinger, of South Lebanon.
   On the 25th, Mr. Peter Gockley, with Miss Susanna Reinhold, both of Cocalico, Lancaster County.
   On the 11th of October, by the Rev. A. B. Schenkel, Mr. John Majer, of Schuylkill County, with Miss Josephine Hoffman, of Lebanon.
   On the 27th of October, by the Rev. Mr. Mauger, Mr. John J. Atkins, with Miss Louisa Forry, both of this city [Lebanon].
   On the day named [October 27], by the Rev. John N. Hoffman, Mr. David Hugh, with Miss Emeline Achenbach, both of Lebanon County.
   On the 27th, Mr. Samuel Klingler, with Miss Amanda Boyer, both of Lebanon.

                  November 11, 1853

Married. On the 8th of this month, by the Rev. Mr. Wedekind, Mr. George M. Faber, with Miss Louisa Siegrist, both of this city [Lebanon].
   On the day named [November 8], by the same, [Rev. Wedekind], Mr. Jeremiah E. Daugherty, of the city of Lebanon, with Miss Lydia Kremer, of Colebrooke.
   On the 3rd of this month, by the Rev. F. W. Kremer, Mr. George Henning of South Annville, with Miss Elisabeth Stein of Pinegrove, Schuylkill County.
   On the 30th of October, by the Rev. T. J. Yeager, Mr. Elias Riddel of South Lebanon Township, with Miss Leah Burkholder of Jackson Township.

                  November 18, 1853

Married. On the 10th of this month, by the Rev. Aug. C. Wedekind, Mr. Joseph Brechbill, with Miss Catharina Fry, both of Belleview [Bellegrove], Lebanon County.

Der Libanon Demokrat                              Lebanon, Pa.

## November 18, 1853 Continued

Married. On the 10 of this month, by the Rev. F. W. Kremer, Mr. John Schirk, of North Annville, with Miss Eliza Hostetter, of South Annville Township.
    On the 13th of this month, by the same [Rev. F. W. Kremer], Mr. Jonas Umberger, with Miss Lucetta Zeller, both of North Lebanon Township.

## November 25, 1853

Married. On the 13th of October, by the Rev. Mr. Laitzel, Mr. Paul Lengel, with Miss Catharina Rohland, both of Hanover, Dauphin County.
    On the 17th of this month, by the Rev. Mr. Jung, Mr. John Licht [Light], of South Lebanon Township, with Miss Maria Guth, of Highspire, Dauphin County.
    By the Rev. Mr. Stein.
    On the 10th of this month, Mr. George Spannuth, with Miss Elisabeth Troutman, both of Jackson Township.
    On the day named [November 10], Mr. Samuel Deininger, with Miss Elisabeth Wallmer, both of East Hanover Township.
    On the 17th of this month, Mr. Michael Groff, of Bethel Township, Lebanon County, with Miss Sarah Kurtz, of Franklin County.
    On the day named, Mr. John Batdorf, of Jackson Township, with Miss Elisabeth Glick, of Bethel Township.
    On the day named, Mr. John Uhrich, with Prescilla Schwarz, both of Jackson Township.
    On the day named, Mr. George Lutz, with Miss Catharina Conrad, both of Bethel Township.
    On the 19th of this month, Mr. Gideon Batz, of Bethel Township, Berks County, with Miss Maria Braumiller, of Bethel Township, Lebanon County.
    On the 10th of this month, by the Rev. L. G. Eggers, Mr. Friedrich Foltz, with Miss Maria Matilda Brehm, both of Jackson Township.
    On the 17th of this month, by the Rev. Aug. C. Wedekind, Mr. Jacob Lang, of South Annville, with Miss Maria Schmidt, of South Lebanon Township.
    On the 17th of this month, by the Rev. T. J. Yeager, Mr. Michael Groh, with Miss Susanna Burkholder, both of Jackson Township.

## December 2, 1853

Married. On the 24th of November, by the Rev. F. W. Kremer, Mr. Adam Hauk, with Miss Rosanna G. Reinhard, both of this city.

Der Libanon Demokrat                                   Lebanon, PA.

### December 2, 1853 Continued

Married. By the Rev. Mr. Stein.
On the 20th of November, Mr. Jacob Lentz, with Miss Catharina Dubs, both of Bethel Township.
On the 24th of November, Mr. Daniel Herschberger, with Miss Elisabeth Runkel, both of North Annville Township.
On the day named [November 24], Mr. Emanuel Lasch, of Union Township, with Miss Sarah Daub, of North Lebanon Township.
On the day named [November 24], Mr. Enos Steiner, with Miss Catharina Brechbill, both of Hanover Township, Dauphin County.
On the 6th of October, by the Rev. Mr. Romich, Mr. Josia Roth, of Dauphin County, with Miss Maria Anna Stiles, of East Hanover, Lebanon County.
On the 9th, by the same, Mr. Thomas Koons, with Miss Prescilla Lingel, both of Dauphin County.
On Thursday, the 1st of this month, by the Rev. Mr. Kremer, Samuel R. Faber, with Miss CAtharina Guth, both of this city.

### December 9, 1853

Married. On Thursday, the 1st of this month, by the Rev. Kramer, Mr. Samuel Faber, with Miss CAtharina Guth, both of this city.
By the Rev. R. S. Wagner, on the 29th of November, Mr. Henry Landis, of Derry, Dauphin County, with Miss Sarah M. Becker, of South Lebanon Township.
By the Rev. Thomas H. Leinbach, Mr. John Hibschman, of Jackson Township, with Miss Sarah Bamberger, of South Lebanon Township.
On the 15th of November, Mr. George Streack, with Miss Sarah Diehl, both of Jackson Township.
On the 20th, Mr. Joseph Lauser, merchant, of Schaefferstown, with Miss Susanna Meck, both of Lebanon County.

### December 16, 1853

Married. By the Rev. J. Stein.
On the 27th of November, Mr. Adam Kerchner, with Miss Delila Meier, both of Union Township.
On the 4th of this month, Mr. William Kniesel, of Jonestown, with Miss Catharina Artz, of Bethel Township.
On the 8th of this month, Mr. David Wendling, of Hanover Township, with Miss Louisa Miller, of North Annville Township.
On the day named [December 8], Mr. Peter H. Freylinghaus, with Miss Anna Elisabeth Schod, of Bethel Township.

Der Libanon Demokrat                    Lebanon, Pa.

December 16, 1853 Continued

Married. On the 4th of this month, by the Rev. Mr. Schrop, Mr. Christian Schaffer, with Mrs. Polly Fernsler, both of this city [Lebanon].
On the 8th of this month, by the same [Rev. Schrop], Mr. Jacob Peffley, of Swatara Township, with Miss Rebecca Ritschert, of North Lebanon Township.

December 30, 1853

Married. On the 11th of this month, by the Rev. G. S. Petri, Mr. Johann Fesig, with Miss Angelina Schwarz, both of Fredericksburg, Lebanon County.
On the 6th of last November, by the same [Rev. G. S. Petri], Mr. Jacob Wagner, with Miss Catharina Faber, both of the above place.
On the 8th of this month, by the Rev. Mr. Bollinger, Mr. Daniel Klein, of North Lebanon, with Miss Sarah Ann Koons, of East Hanover Township.
On the 11th of December, by the Rev. J. STein, Mr. Nathaniel Berlot, with Miss Savilla Waltermartin, both of Swatara Township.
On the 29th of this month, by the Rev. J. STein, Mr. Johannes Loser, with Miss Sarah Ellen Thompson, both of Swatara Township.
By the Rev. Thomas H. Leinbach.
On the 8th of this month, Mr. Elias Etris, with Miss Elisabeth Wolf, both of Bethel Township, Lebanon County.
On the 10th, Mr. Peter B. Knoebel, of Bethel Township, Berks County, with Miss Susanna Albert, of Bethel Township, Lebanon County.
On the 15th, Mr. Samuel Burkholder, of West Cocalico, Lancaster County, with Miss Catharina Schnebely, of Heidelberg, Lebanon County.
On the 24th, Mr. William H. Zerbe, with Miss Carolina Leintner, both of Millersburg, Berks County.
On the 22nd of this month, by the Rev. John M. Hoffman, Mr. Abraham Foreman, with Miss Catharina Stauffer, both of Lebanon County.
On the 25th of this month, by the same [Rev. John M. Hoffman], Mr. Michael K. Burkholder, with Miss Barbara Ann Reist, both of South Lebanon Township.
On the 22nd of this month, by the Rev. F. W. Kremer, Mr. Montgomery Hughes, with Miss Mary A. Yeager, both of Dauphin County.
On the 26th of this month, Mr. Henry Missimer, with Miss Martha Riehm, both of Schaefferstown.

January 6, 1854

Married. On the 29th of December, by the Rev. F. W. Kre-

Der Libanon Demokrat                          Lebanon, Pa.

### January 6, 1854 Continued

Mr. Isaac R. Kehl, with Miss Sarah Ann Gerhart, both of this city [Lebanon].
    On the 3rd of this month, by the Rev. Aug. C. Wedekind, Mr. Edward Klein, of Mechanicsville, Dauphin County, with Miss Eliza Miller, of East Hanover, Lebanon County.
    On the 3rd of this month, Mr. Joseph B. Albert, of East Hanover, Dauphin County, with Elizabeth Kreider, of East Hanover, Lebanon County.
    On the 26th of December, by the Rev. Mr. Carper, Henry Herschberger, of Union Township, with Miss Mary Ann Crick, of South Annville.

### January 13, 1854

Married. On the 26th of December, by the Rev. Mr. Romig, Mr. Rudolph Endesberger, with Miss Johanna Fredericka Kessling, both of Jonestown.
    On the 3rd of this month, by the same [Rev. Romig], Mr. Adam Sattazahn, with Miss Catharina Gress.
    On the 8th of this month, by the Rev. John M. Hoffman, Mr. John Hegele, with Miss Hannah Folmer, both of North Lebanon.

### January 20, 1854

Married. On the 15th of this month, by the Rev. Mr. Schrop, Mr. William Black, of North Annville, with Miss Mary Reidel, of North Lebanon.
    On the 12th of this month, by the Rev. Mr. Kremer, Mr. Henry Buch, of this city, with Miss Leah Ginter, of York County.
    On the 20th of December, by the Rev. R. S. Wagner, Mr. Andreas Zimmerman, of South Lebanon Township, with Miss Maria Landis, of Derry, Dauphin County.
    On the 20th of December, by the Rev. C. Hummel, Mr. William Noun, of Lancaster County, with Miss Maria Anna Miller, of Lebanon County.
    On the 8th of January, Mr. Tobias W. Garberig, with Miss Lavina Anna R. Deininger, both of East Hanover Township.

### January 27, 1854

Married. On the 8th of this month, by the Rev. Mr. Sapper, Mr. John Gratz, with Rebecca Leffler, both of Union Township.
    On the 14th, by the same [Rev. Sapper], Mr. Cyrus Mies, with Miss Esther Puhr, both of Union Township.
    On the 21st, by the same [Rev. Sapper], Mr. Joseph Walter of Bethel, with Miss Rosina Fehg, of Union.

Der Libanon Demokrat                                Lebanon, Pa.

              January 27, 1854 Continued

Married. On the 3rd of this month, by the Rev. T. H. Leinbach, Mr. John Reats, with Miss Catharina Hagi [Heagy], both of Cocalico Township, Lancaster County.
     On the 19th, by the same [Rev. T. H. Leinbach], Mr. Jacob Gockley, with Miss Eliza Zimmerman, both of Millcreek.
     On the 23rd, by the same [Rev. T. H. Leinbach], Mr. George Lindenmuth, with Miss Lydia Dinges, both of Myerstown.

                February 3, 1854

Married. On the 26th of January, by the Rev. Mr. Stein, George Ruhl, with Susanna Lutz, both of North Lebanon Township. - On the 26th, by the same [Rev. Stein], Mr. Jonathan Dubs, with Matilda Gundrum, both of Bethel Township, Lebanon County.
     On the 28th of January, by the Rev. Aug. Wedekind, Mr. Ludwig Fischer, Jr., of Heidelberg, Berks County, with Ann Eliza Schmaltz, of Jackson Township, Lebanon County.
     On the 10th of January, by the Rev. Mr. Hiester, Mr. Reuben Long, with Miss Amelie Peter, both of Londonderry Township.

                February 10, 1854

Married. on the 2nd of this month, by the Rev. E. W. Hutter, Mr. John G. Schirk, with Miss Susan Matilda Goschart, both of this city [Lebanon].

                February 17, 1854

Married. On the 28th of January, by the Rev. T. H. Leinbach, Mr. Daniel Schneider, with Miss Emilia Pfeifer, both of Bethel Township.
     On the 21st of this month, by the same [Rev. T. H. Leinbach], Mr. Henry Virler, with Miss Sarah Jane M'Curty, both of South Lebanon. - On the day named [February 2], by the same [Rev. T. H. Leinbach], Mr. William Weirich, of Jackson, with Miss Magdalena Spitler, of Bethel. - Likewise, Mr. William Oxenreider with Miss Melinda Henriette Boyer, both of Jackson.

                February 25, 1854

Married. On the 16th of this month, by the Rev. J. R. Hoffman, Mr. John Smith, with Miss Maria Brandt, both of Lebanon.

Der Libanon Demokrat                    Lebanon, Pa.

February 25, 1854 Continued

Married. On the 15th of this month, by the Rev. Mr. Mauger, Mr. John Miller, with Miss Wilmina Hartman, both of Lebanon.
On the 14th of this month, by the Rev. Mr. Wedekind, Mr. George Weidman, of Belleview [Bellegrove], with Miss Parmilla Heilman, of Jonestown.

March 3, 1854

Married. On the 19th of February, by the Rev. Mr. Sapper, Mr. Jonathan Anspach, with Sarah Ann Hartman, both of Union Township.
On the 2nd of February, by the Rev. A. J. Strine, Mr. Monroe H. Mullen, of Ohio, formerly of Lancaster County, with Miss Mary Ann Schucker, of Schaefferstown, Lebanon County.
On the 9th of February, by the Rev. A. Romich, Mr. Joel Grate, of the city of Lebanon, with Miss Elisabeth Fuchs, of Swatara Township.
On the 14th of February, by the same [Rev. A. Romich], Mr. Levi Corl, with Miss Lydia Schitz, both of East Hanover.

March 17, 1854

Married. On the 2nd of March, by the Rev. Mr. Romich, Mr. Solomon Raab, with Rebecca Fischer, both of East Hanover.
On the 22nd of February, by the Rev. Mr. Stein, Mr. Elias Kreiser, with Miss Catharine Weiss, both of Union Township.

March 24, 1854

Married. On the 27th of February, by the Rev. Johann R. Kleinfelter, Mr. Mack Beck, with Miss Maria Felty, both of Millcreek Township.
On the 12th of March, by the Rev. Mr. Siegrist, Mr. Henry Diemer, with Miss Anna Mathues, both of Heidelberg Township.
On the 19th of this month, by the Rev. Mr. Kremer, Mr. Jacob Spangler, widower, with Miss Mary Rohland, both of South Lebanon Township.
On the 16th of this month, by the Rev. H. B. Mauger, Mr. James Gerret, with Miss Fanny Donley, both of Cornwall, Lebanon County.
On the 19th of this month, by the same [Rev. H. B. Mauger], Mr. Caspr McConnell, of the city of Lebanon, with Miss Barbara Schay, of North Lebanon.

Der Libanon Demokrat                    Lebanon, Pa.

### April 7, 1854

Married. On the 30th of March, by the Rev. F. W. Kremer, Mr. Tobias Derkes, with Miss Catharina Hammer, both of this city [Lebanon].

### May 23, 1856

Married. On the 18th of May, by the Rev. Mr. Stein, Mr. Wilhelm Mertz, with Miss Catharina Klein, both of Bernville, Berks County.
On the 18th of May, by the Rev. Johann R. Kleinfelter, Mr. Johann Weil, with Miss Elisabeth Balm, both of Heidelberg Township, Lebanon County.

### May 30, 1856

Married. On the 9th of this month, by the Rev. J. E. Hiester, Mr. John Trump, with Miss Elmira Rieth, both of Annville.
On the 20th of this month, by the same [Rev. J. E. Hiester], Mr. Stephen W. Boltz, of North Annville, with Miss Fanny R. Wagner, of East Hanover.
On the 25th of this month, by the same [Rev. J. E. Hiester], Mr. John Hoffman, of Londonderry with Mrs. Sarah Zügler [Ziegler], of Derry Township, Dauphin County.

### June 6, 1856

Married. On the 29th of May, by the Rev. Friedrich Kreider, Mr. Asaph Licht [Light], of Lebanon, with Miss Catharina Schneider of Schaefferstown.
On the 29th of May, by the Rev. J. Stein, Mr. Israel Walborn, of Dauphin County, with Miss Lydia Ettris [Edris], of Bethel Township, Lebanon County.
On the 1st of this month, by the Rev. Aug. C. Wedekind, Mr. Henry W. Miller, with MIss Sarah Strickler, both of Schaefferstown.
On the 1st of this month, by the Rev. H. S. Miller, George W. Kain, of Ottawa, Ill., with Miss Mary Ann Gingrich of Lebanon.

### June 13, 1856

Married. On the 1st of this month, by C. D. Zehring, Esq., Mr. Jacob Getz, with Miss Eliza Kreiser, both of Union Township.
On the 3rd of June, by the Rev. S. G. Rhoads, at Beartown, Lancaster County, the honorable James D. Lehr, of Dauphin County, with Miss Catharina Anna Miesse, of Schaefferstown.

Der Libanon Demokrat                               Lebanon, Pa.

June 13, 1856 Continued

Married. On the 16th of April, in Ottawa, LaSalle County, Ill., by the Rev. Mr. Forre, Mr. Henry Shaw, of Ottawa, with Miss Mary L. Keim, of Ottawa, formerly of North Lebanon Borough.
    On the 8th of June, by the Rev. F. W. Kremer, Mr. Cornelius C. Gerhart, with Miss Anna Caldwell, both of this city [Lebanon].
    On the 9th of March, by the Rev. Lerch, Mr. John Elliot, Jr., formerly of Lebanon, with Miss Margaret Walters, of Lasalle Township, Monroe County, Michigan.

June 20, 1856

Married. On the 12th of June, by the Rev. Johannes Stein, Mr. Jacob Seltzer, with Miss Chris Kreiser, both of Hanover Township, Lebanon County.
    On the 14th of June, by the same [Rev. Johannes Stein], Mr. Johannes Kaufman, with Miss Maria Schafer, both of Jackson Township, Lebanon County.
    On the 15th of June, by the same [Rev. Johannes Stein], Mr. Samuel K. Derkes, with Adleine Bird, both of Union Township.

June 27, 1856

Married. On the 18th of June, by the Rev. F. W. Kremer, Mr. Charles Davis of Reading, with Miss Hannah Foreman of Reading Furnace, Pa.

July 4, 1856

Married. On the 29th of June, by the Rev. F. W. Kremer, Mr. Peter Weirich, of North Lebanon, with Miss Maria Bleistein, of South Lebanon Township.
    On the same day [June 29], by the same [Rev. F. W. Kremer], Mr. William Hege with widow Mary Roberts, both of Cornwall, Lebanon County.
    On the 26th of June, by the Rev. Aug. C. Wedekind, Mr. Thomas Boger with Susan Foltz, both of Annville.

July 25, 1856

Married. On the 17th of June, by the Rev. H. S. Miller, John P. Kehl, of Lebanon, wuth Amanda S. Stroh, of Annville.
    On the day named [June 17], by the same [Rev. H. S. Miller], John Pflieger, with Sophia Miller, both of North Lebanon.
    On the day named [June 17], by the same [Rev. H. S. Miller], John Diemer, with Helen Holsem, both of North

Der Libanon Demokrat						Lebanon, Pa.

July 25, 1856

Married. On the 17th of this month, by the Rev. H. S. Miller, John P. Kehl, of Lebanon, with Amanda S. Stroh, of Annville.
On the day named [July 17], by the same [Rev. H. S. Miller], John Pflieger, with Sophia Miller, both of North Lebanon.
On the day named [July 17], by the same [Rev. H. S. Miller], John Diemer, with Helena Holsem, both of North Lebanon.
On the day named [July 17], by the same [Rev. H. S. Miller], Christian Demler, with Maria Holsem, both of North Lebanon.

August 1, 1856

Married. On the 5th of July, by the Rev. Mr. Stein, Christian Schäd [Shade], with Ellen Hartlein, both of Jonestown, Lebanon County.
On the 10th of July, by the same [Rev. Stein], George Henninger, with Miss Leah Sattezahn, both of Jackson Township.
On the 20th of July, Jacob Hedrich, with Miss Rebecca Becker, both of West Hanover, Dauphin County.
On the 27th, Johannes Brand, with Lydia Reifein, both of North Lebanon Township.

August 8, 1856

Married. On the 31st of July, by the Rev. J. S. Cook, Joseph Kauffman, with Ann Binner, both of Cornwall.
On the 20th of July, by the Rev. Samuel Bingling, Samuel Miller, with Emmaline Lease, both of Londonderry Township, Lebanon County.

August 22, 1856

Married. On the 3rd of August, by the Rev. Mr. Stein, William Donly, of South Lebanon Township, with Miss Carolina Neu, of Hanover Township, Lebanon County.
On the 10th of August, by the same [Rev. Stein], William Boeshore, with Priscilla Miess, both of Union Township.
On the 14th, by the same, Mr. Jacob Wengert, of South Hanover Township, Dauphin County, with Elisabeth Licht [Light], of North Lebanon Township.
In the city of Philadelphia, on last Thursday morning, [August 14], by the Rev. John McDowell, Mrs. Annie C. Parker, daughter of Mr. Joseph Craig, of Philadelphia with the Rev. John N. Hoffman, pastor of the Trinity Lutheran Church, Reading

Der Libanon Demokrat                                 Lebanon, Pa.

### August 22, 1856 Continued

Married. On the 26th of this month, by the Rev. John Gring, Peter Sattezahn, of this county, with Mrs. Rebecca Luckenbill, of Schuylkill County.

On Tuesday, July 22nd, by the Rev. Mr. Koble, Mr. Jacob Miller, of Dayton, Ohio, formerly of Annville, Pa., with Miss Mary A. Dow, of East Concord, Bureau County, Illinois.

### August 29, 1856

Married. On the 14th of this month, by the Rev. John R. Kleinfelter, Mr. Stevens Schilling, with Miss Catharina Christman, both of Millcreek Township, Lebanon County.

On the 18th of this month, by A. S. Ely, Esq., Thomas O'Connel with Catharina Hortnent, both of Lebanon County.

On the 12th of this month, in Mercersburg, by the Rev. Thomas Creigh, Mr. Daniel Heilman, of Annville, Lebanon County, with Ellen C. Scully, of Mercersburg, Franklin County.

On the 5th of this month, in Chilicothe, by the Rev. Carson, Benjamin Bicher, formerly of this city [Lebanon], with Libbia A. Patterson, of Camp Charlotte, Pickaway County, Ohio.

### September 5, 1856

Married. On the 24th of August, by the Rev. Mr. Stein, Mr. Isaac Sanderson with Miss Maria Schucker, both of Jonestown, Lebanon County.

On the 30th, by the same [Rev. Stein], Mr. Joseph Daub, with Miss Eliza Schadel, both of Jackson Township.

On the 28th, by the Rev. Mr. Miller, Mr. John Mauty, of Union Township, with Lodia Kremer, of North Lebanon Township.

On the 30th, by the same [Rev. Miller], George Uhler, of North Lebanon, with Elizabeth Dixon, of this borough.

On the 28th, by the Rev. Mr. Kremer, Abraham Lehman, of Lancaster County, with Anna Sheets, of Dauphin County.

On the 31st, by the same [Rev. Kremer], Mr. Abraham Brandt, of Lancaster County, with Susan Ebrecht of Lebanon County.

On the 2nd of this month, in this city [Lebanon], by the Rev. Mr. Miller, Mr. Emanuel Weidman, of Clay Township, with Miss Lovina Zartman, of Elisabeth Township, both of Lancaster County.

On the day named [September 2], in the city of Lancaster, Peter Zartman, of Elisabeth Township, with Sarah Wachter, of Clay Township, Lancaster County.

Der Libanon Demokrat                              Lebanon, Pa.

                    September 12, 1856

Married. On the 30th of August, by the Rev. F. W. Kremer, John F. Schaffner, of Middletown, Dauphin County, with Catharine Holsberg, of North Annville, Lebanon County.
        On the 2nd of this month, in this city [Lebanon], by the Rev. F. W. Kremer, P. Stein, of Muscatine, Iowa, with Miss Annie E. Siegrist, of this city [Lebanon].
        On the day named [September 2], by the same [Rev. F. W. Kremer], William R. Schmith, _____, with Elizabeth, daughter of Mr. Abraham Licht [Light], all of this city [Lebanon].
        On the 4th of this month, by the Rev. August C. Wedekind, Samuel Schrom, of Schaefferstown, with Mary Good, of Hummelstown, Dauphin County.
        On the 9th of this month, by the same, John A. Boger, of Harrisburg, with Mary A. Kuhnle, of Annville.

                    September 12, 1856

Married. On the 9th of this month, by the Rev. F. W. Kremer, Abraham Hostetter, of Annville, with Louisa Meck, of North Annville.
        On the day named [September 9], by the same [Rev. F. W. Kremer], Daniel Lutz, with Sarah Binckley, both of Lancaster County.
        On the 4th of this month, in Wayne County, Ohio, by the Rev. Mr. Smith, Moses Grove, with Mary Hostetter, formerly of North Lebanon Township.
        On the 11th of this month, by the Rev. H. S. Miller, William Blauch, of Lebanon, with Mary Stover, of Cornwall.
        On the 4th of this month, by the Rev. J. M. Ditzler, Isaac Ulrich, of Warwick Township, Lancaster County, with Rosianna Biemerderfer, of Heidelberg Township, Lebanon County.
        On the day named [September 4], by the same [Rev. J. M. Ditzler], Cyrus Minnig with Maria Ruth, both of Schoeneck, Lancaster County.
        On the 11th of this month, Mr. Levi Maulfair, with Miss Rebecca Van Reed, both of North Annville.

                    September 26, 1856

Married. On the 18th of this month, by the Rev. J. E. Hiester, Mr. Isaac Ellinger, of Union Deposit, Dauphin County, with Miss Caroline Riem of Annville.
        On the same day [September 18], by the same [Rev. J. E. Hiester], Mr. Jacob Dutweiler, of South Annville, with Miss Eliza Kettering, of Palmyra.

Der Libanon Demokrat                    Lebanon, Pa.

September 26, 1856 Continued

Married. On the same day [September 18], by the same [Rev. J. E. Hiester], Mr. Henry Martin, with Miss Mary Ann Bender, both of Annville.
On the 21st of this month, by the Rev. H. S. Miller, Mr. Andrew Gerberich, of North Lebanon, with Miss Elisabeth Horst of this city [Lebanon].
On the 29th of June, by the Rev. Mr. Jacobs, Mr.· John Miller, of Philadelphia, with Miss Sarah Embich, of Lebanon.

October 3, 1856

Married. On the 24th of September, by the Rev. Samuel Yingling, Mr. Joseph Gerberich, with Miss Elizabeth Snoke, both of Palmyra, Lebanon County.
On the 4th of September, by the same, Mr. William H. H. Embich, with Miss Hannah R. Wagner, both of this city [Lebanon].
On the 18th of this month, by the Rev. Mr. Lieve Herzler, George Klein of Tulpehocken Township, Berks County, with Miss Catharina Senner, of Lancaster County.

Occtober 10, 1856

Married. On the 2nd of this month, by the Rev. Miller, Mr. Henry Mertz, with Maria Wagner, both of North Lebanon.
On the 5th of this month, by the Rev. F. W. Kremer, Mr. Herman J. Hambleton, of Cornwall, with Miss Sarah Lasch, of this city [Lebanon].
On the 1st of this month, by the Rev. William Groh, Dr. John R. Krum, of Schaefferstown, with Mary Ann Miller, of Brickerville, Lancaster County.

October 17, 1856

Married. On the 18th of September, by the Rev. Mr. Stein, Mr. Josiah Donmoyer, of Swatara, with Miss Magdalena Hess of Union Township.
On the 27th, by the same [Rev. Stein], Mr. Jacob Meily, of Bethel Township, with Susanna Schul, of Union Township, Lebanon County.
On the 2nd of October, by the same [Rev. Stein], Mr. Johannes Rittel, with Susanna Brechbill, both of Bethel Township, Lebanon County.
On the day named [October 2], by the same [Rev. Stein], Mr. Joseph Yordy, with Anna Brechbill, both of Hanover, Lebanon County.

Der Libanon Demokrat                    Lebanon, Pa.

October 24, 1856

Married. On the 2nd of September, by the Rev. Mr. Siegrist, Mr. Daniel Karl, of East Hempfield, Lancaster County, with Miss Catharina Saylor, of Elizabeth Furnace, Lancaster County.
 On the 14th of September, by the same [Rev. Siegrist], Mr. Adam Noll, of Heidelberg, with Miss Polly Heinly, of West Cocalico, Lancaster County.
 On the 8th of October, by the Rev. Mr. Stein, Mr. Jeremias Gassert, of Lononderry Township, Lebanon County, with Amanda Stehly, of Hanover, Dauphin County.
 On the 12th of October, by the same [Rev. Stein], Jonas Teis, with Henrietta Wittemeyer, both of Bethel Township, Lebanon County.
 On the 3rd of this month, by Joseph R. Henry, Esq., Mr. John Fronk, with Miss Susan Leadum, both of South Annville Township, Lebanon County.
 On the 18th of September, by the same [Joseph R. Henry, Esq.], Mr. John Murry, with Miss Mary Brandt, both of Cornwall Township.
 On the 16th of this month, by the Rev. H. S. Miller, Henry Pfautz with Sarah Kreider, both of Lancaster County.
 On the 17th of this month, by the Rev. F. W. Kremer, Mr. Charles P. Moyer, of this city [Lebanon], with Miss Clara S. Seltzer, of Womelsdorf, Berks County.

October 31, 1856

Married. On the 23rd of this month, by the Rev. H. S. Miller, George Gemi, with Mary Hoke, both of Cornwall.
 On the 21st of this month, by the Rev. F. W. Kremer, Mr. Jerome S. Weaber, of Fredericksburg, with Miss Lizzie M. Rise, of this city [Lebanon].
 On the 16th of this month, by the Rev. J. E. Hiester, Cosmus Clendenin, with Miss Lucinda W. Fox, both of Derry Township, Dauphin County.
 On the same day [October 16], by the same [Rev. J. E. Hiester], Mr. Elijah Maulfair, with Miss Louisa Urich, both of North Annville.
 On the same day [October 16], by the same [Rev. J. E. Hiester], Mr. Jacob F. Hemperly, of Londonderry, with Miss Catharina Miller, of East Hanover, Lebanon County.
 On the same day [October 16], by the same [Rev. J. E. Hiester], Mr. Henry Leineweber, with Miss Mary Troxel, both of Annville.
 On the 30th of this month, by the Rev. J. E. Hiester, Mr. Reuben Heilman, with Miss Sarah Biever, both of Annville.
 On the same day [October 30], by the same [Rev. J. E. Hiester], Mr. Joseph Peter, with Miss Clarisa Nafzger, both of Annville.

Der Libanon Demokrat                                                  Lebanon, Pa.

### November 7, 1856

Married. By the Rev. Mr. Stein
On the 19th of October, David Rittel, of North Lebanon, with Ellen Bensing, of Bethel Township, Berks County.

On the 23rd of October, John Heinrich Kohr, of Bethel Township, Lebanon County, with Hanna Scherg, of Union Township, Lebanon County.

On the 30th of October, George Gerling, of Union Township, Lebanon County, with Sara Gehret, of Bethel Township, Berks County.

### November 14, 1856

Married. On the 20th of October, by the Rev. Mr. Gring, Thomas Snyder, of Chester County, with Sara Anna G. Miller, of Lebanon.

On the 6th of this month, by the Rev. F. W. Kremer, Jesse Gerhart, with Christiana Bechtel, both of this city [Lebanon].

On the 9th of this month, by the same [Rev. F. W. Kremer], Henry W. Eby, with Kesiah Stump, both of South Lebanon Township, this county.

On the 9th of this month, by the Rev. H. S. Miller, John Louch, with Mary Witmeyer, both of this city [Lebanon].

On the 6th of this month, by the Rev. H. S. Miller, George Kapp, with Frederica Albrecht, both of North Lebanon.

On the 9th of this month, by the Rev. Aug. C. Wedekind, John K. Karch, with Harriet S. George, both of this city [Lebanon].

On the 30th of October, in Springville, Stephenson County, Illinois, by the Rev. J. M. Sindlinger, Edwin Carl Duth, with Miss Sarah A. Reissner, formerly of this city [Lebanon].

### November 21, 1856

Married. On the 11th of November, by the Rev. Stein, James L. Allen, with Elisabeth Bauman, both of West Hanover, Dauphin County.

On the 16th, by the same [Rev. Stein], Heinrich Artz, of Bethel Township, Berks County, with Elisabeth Wolf, of Bethel Township, Lebanon County.

On the 2nd of this month, by the Rev. T. H. Leinbach, Mr. Samuel Markey, of Schaefferstown, with Miss Susanna Schwanger, of Jackson Township.

On the 6th, by the same [Rev. T. H. Leinbach], Jeremiah Fiess, with Miss Eliza Gotwalt, both of Jackson Township, Lebanon County. - Likewise Samuel White with Catharina Grumlauf, both of Lancaster County.

Der Libanon Demokrat                           Lebanon, Pa.

November 21, 1856 Continued

Married. On the 11th by the same [Rev. T. H. Leinbach], Joseph A. Leinbach (Merchant), of Jackson Township, Lebanon County, with Miss Amelia A. Keiser, of Marion Township, Berks County.

On the 13th, by the same [Rev. T. H. Leinbach], Mr. Jefferson Muth, with Miss Sarah Ann Haak, both of Jackson Township, Lebanon County.

On the 16th of November, by the Rev. Friedrich Krocker, John B. Walter, with Margaretha North, both of Millcreek Township, Lebanon County.

On the 10th of this month, by the Rev. Aug. C. Wedekind, Levi Brant, of Dauphin County, with Mary Ann Mummaw, of Londonderry Township.

On the day named [November 10], by the same [Rev. Aug. C. Wedekind], Christian S. Bomberger, with Eliza Fessler, both of South Lebanon.

On the 13th of this month, by the Rev. F. W. Kremer, Isaac Stout, of this city [Lebanon], with Catharine Reed, of North Lebanon Borough.

On the 9th of this month, by the Rev. Mr. Cook, Edwin Miller, with Susan Gerdy, both of this city [Lebanon].

November 28, 1856

Married. On the 11th of this month, by the Rev. J. E. Hiester, Benjamin Peter with Miss Sarah Rupp, both of North Annville.

On the 13th of this month, by the Rev. Samuel Yingling, Joseph Kremer with Miss Susan B. Lessley, both of Londonderry Township, Lebanon County.

On the day named [November 13], by the same [Rev. Samuel Yingling], George Hemperly with Elizabeth Biecher, both of Londonderry Township.

On the 13th of this month, by the same [Rev. Samuel Yingling], Michael Horst with Miss Elizabeth Ellinger, both of Londonderry Township.

On the 6th of this month, by the Rev. Gring, Abraham U. Scherk, of Swatara Township, with Miss Mary Hedrich, of Union Township.

December 5, 1856

Married. On the 27th of November, by the Rev. H. S. Miller, John Krebel, with Catharine Getz, both of Lebanon.

On the 27th of November, by the Rev. J. M. Ditzler, Dr. L. Baddorf, with Mary Anna Spangler, both of Wohleberstown [Mt. Aetna], Berks County, Pa.

On the 12th of November, in Indianapolis, Indiana, by the Rev. Mr. Stevenson, Dr. W. Moore Guilford, of Lebanon, Pa., with Miss Ann Mary Elder, of Indianapolis.

Der Libanon Demokrat                    Lebanon, Pa.

December 5, 1856 Continued

Married. On the 9th of November, by the Rev. A. Romich, Mr. John Schally, with Miss Barbara Umberger, both of Swatara.
    On the 13th of November, by the same, Mr. Henry Lingle with Miss Caroline Lerch, both of East Hanover, Dauphin County.
    On the 27th of November, by the Rev. A. S. Leinbach, William Eckert, of North Lebanon, with Miss Rosanna Kleiser, of Cornwall, Lebanon County.

December 12, 1856

Married. On the 20th of November, by the Rev. Samuel Yingling, Israel G. Ward, formerly of North Annville, Lebanon County (last of Ohio), with Ellen G. Snoddy, of Derry Township, Dauphin County.
    On the 27th of November, by the same, Cyrus Keath, with Mary Lessley, both of Londonderry.
    On the day named [November 27], by the same, Aaron Swartley, of Lebanon, with Mary Kreider, of Londonderry.
    On the 2nd of this month, by the Rev. F. W. Kremer, Jacob Brubacher with Mary Dissinger, both of South Lebanon Township.
    On the 7th of this month, by the same [Rev. F. W. Kremer], Henry Schroff, of South Lebanon Township, with Mary Licht [Light], of Hanover, this county.
    On the 27th of November, by the Rev. Mr. Reinbold, Mr. Moses S. Klein, of South Lebanon Township, with Miss Elizabeth Hollinger, of Derry Township, Dauphin County.

December 19, 1856

Married. On the 14th of this month, by the Rev. F. W. Kremer, John J. Klick, of Cornwall Township, with Miss Mary, daughter of Michael Kreider of this city [Lebanon].
    On the 9th of this month, by the Rev. J. S. Cook, John Hare, of Montreal, Canada, with Hannah C., daughter of Thomas McLahe, of Cornwall Township, Lebanon County.
    On the 11th of this month, by the Rev. H. S. Miller, Jacob Keller, with Mrs. Maria Margaret Reichman.
    On the 4th of this month, by the Rev. Mr. Gring, Mr. William Tobias, with Malinda Gettel, both of Fredericksburg, Lebanon County.

December 26, 1856

Married. On the 13th of November, by the Rev. J. E. HIester, Mr. Michael Horst, with Miss Elizabeth Ellinger, both of Londonderry.

Der Libanon Demokrat                    Lebanon, Pa.

December 26, 1856 Continued

Married. On the 4th of December, by the same [Rev. J. E. Hiester], Mr. John Gundreman, with Miss Katharina Kreider, both of South Annville.

On the 30th of November, by the Rev. A. Reinbold, Mr. John Addison Satezahn, with Miss Magdalena Schally, both of East Hanover, Lebanon County.

On the 4th of December, by the same [Rev. A. Reinbold], Mr. Abraham Albert, with Miss Melinda Deck, both of East Hanover, Lebanon County.

January 2, 1857

Married. On the 23rd of this month, in this city, by the Rev. J. S. Cook, Mr. Henry Waltemyer, of Shrewsbury, Pa., with Miss Sarah Garrett, of Cornwall, this county.

On the 23rd of this month, by the Rev. H. S. Miller, Mr. John Henry Weber, with Miss Leah Shugar, both of this city [Lebanon].

On the 23rd of this month, by the same, Mr. David S. Dotter with Miss Rosanna Seabold, both of South Annville.

On the 18th of this month, by the Rev. F. W. Kremer, Mr. Amos Tittle, of South Annville Township, with Miss Mary Riechert, of this city.

On the 18th of this month, by the Rev. Aug. C. Wedekind, Mr. John Benson, of North Lebanon, with Miss Sarah A. Lantz, of Cornwall.

On the 28th of December, by the Rev. Friedrich Krocker, Elias R. Licht [Light] with Miss Elisabeth H. Schwartz, both of this city [Lebanon].

January 9, 1857

Married. On the 18th of December, by the Rev. H. Leinbach, Mr. Jonathan M. Killmer, with Miss Rebecca Kurr, both of Millersburg, Berks County.

On the day named [December 18], by the same [Rev. H. Leinbach], Mr. George Hay, with Miss Sarah Treist, both of North Lebanon.

On the 21st of December, by the same [Rev. H. Leinbach], Andrew Yuengst, with Elizabeth Brubacher, both of Heidelberg.

On the 25th of December, by the same [Rev. H. Leinbach], Mr. Abraham Krall, with Miss CAtharina Schneider, both of Heidelberg.

On the 1st of January, by the same [Rev. H. Leinbach], Mr. Michael Reynolsen, with Miss Margaretha Derr, both of Jackson Township, all of Lebanon County.

On the 1st of January, by the Rev. Mr. J. Stein, Johannes E. Justen, with Miss Sarah Anna Buchter, both of the city of Lebanon.

Der Libanon Demokrat   Lebanon, Pa.

January 9, 1857 Continued

On the 30th of November, by the Rev. Mr. John Stein, Jacob Riegel, with Amanda Brechbill, both of East Hanover Township, Lebanon County.

On the 13th of December, by the same [Rev. John Stein], David Stover, with Elisabeth Hunsicker, both of Bethel Township, of the aforesaid county.

On the 21st of December, by the same [Rev. John Stein], Josua Miller, with Miss Elisabeth Walter, of Jonestown, in the aforesaid county.

On the 25th of December, by the same [Rev. John Stein], Franklin Schade with Elisabeth Scherk, both of Jonestown.

On the 28th of December, by the same, Johannes Behny, with Maria M'Kinney, both of Union Township, in the aforesaid county.

On the 23rd of December, by the Rev. Mr. Kremer, John H. Ward, of Fredericksburg, with Catharina Fox, of North Lebanon.

On the 24th of December, by the Rev. Mr. Ditzler, James Seibert, with Catharina Bennetum, both of Womelsdorf, Berks County.

On the 25th of December, by the same [Rev. Ditzler], Daniel Degler, of Bethel Township, Berks County, with Sellera Schade, of Upper Tulpehocken, in the aforesaid county.

On the day named [December 25], by the same [Rev. Ditzler], Dr. Samuel Schaffer, with Maryanna Winmoyer, both of Brickerville, in Lancaster County.

On the day named [December 25], by the same [Rev. Ditzler], Josiah Anderson, with Sophia Burky, of Schuylkill Haven.

On the 28th of December, by the same [Rev. Ditzler], George Baer, with Mary Anna Eggenroth, both of Annville.

On the 22nd of December, by the Rev. Samuel Yingling, Jacob L. Hiestand, of Lancaster County, with Anna Howard, of Londonderry Township.

On the 4th of this month, by the Rev. F. W. Kremer, Mr. Reuben Bender, of North Lebanon Boro', with Miss Rosanna Brandt, of this city [Lebanon].

On the 1st of this month, by the Rev. Aug. C. Wedekind, Hiram F. Landis, of Hummelstown, with Miss Mary Landis, of Palmyra.

On the 1st of this month, in this city [Lebanon], by the Rev. H. S. Miller, George Homer, with Sarah Stanly, both of Birdsboro, Berks County.

January 16, 1857

Married. On the 7th of this month, by the Rev. D. R. Miesse, Mr. Isaac Ditzler (widower), with Miss Polly

Der Libanon Demokrat                              Lebanon, Pa.

               January 16, 1857 Continued

Resch, both of Heidelberg Township, Lebanon County.
     On the 6th of this month, by the Rev. Mr. John Zug,
Mr. Joseph P. Gippel, of Heidelberg Township, with Miss
Elisabeth Groh, daughter of Jacob Groh, of Bethel Township, Lebanon County.
     On the 8th of this month, by the Rev. F. W. Kremer,
Abraham Bleistein, of South Lebanon Township, with Catharina Benson, of North Lebanon Township.
     On the 11th of this month, by the same [Rev. F. W.
Kremer], William Meyers, with Sarah Gerret, both of this
city [Lebanon].
     On the 8th of this month, by the Rev. H. S. Miller,
William Bemenderfer, with Miss Susanna Bretz, both of
North Lebanon.

                    January 23, 1857

Married. On the 13th of this month, by the Rev. F. W.
Kremer, Michael Westenberger, of East Hanover, Dauphin
County, with Priscilla Behley, of South Hanover, Dauphin County.
     On the 15th of this month, by the same [Rev. F. W.
Kremer], Joseph Lang, with Mary Ann Schakespeare, both
of Dauphin County.

                    January 30, 1857

Married. On the 22nd of this month, by the Rev. F. W.
Kremer, John Campbell, of this city [Lebanon], with Miss
Mary Miller, of Jonestown.
     On the 8th of this month, by the Rev. Samuel Yingling, John H. Border, of South Annville, with Miss Mary
Snoddy, of Palmyra.

                    February 6, 1857

Married. On the 22nd of January, by the Rev. F. W. Kremer, John Campbell, of this city [Lebanon], with Miss
Mary Miller, of Jonestown.
     On the 8th of January, by the Rev. J. Stein, Mr.
Benjamin Bicksler, with Miss Martha Weber, both of Cumberland County.
     On the 27th of January, by the same [Rev. John Stein],
Johann G. Scherg, with Miss Rebecca Miller, both of Hanover Township, Lebanon County.
     On the 3rd of February, by the same [Rev. John Stein],
Jonathan Miess, with Miss Sophie Adams, both of Swatara
Township, Lebanon County.
     On the day named, [February 3], by the same [Rev.
John Stein], Slm. Baumgartner, with Miss Elisabeth Badorf, both of Hanover Township, Lebanon County.

Der Libanon Demokrat                                Lebanon, Pa.

February 6, 1857 Continued

Married. On the 29th of January, by the Rev. F. W. Kremer, John P. Fessler, of South Lebanon Township, with Miss Joanna Bowman, of Cornwall Township.
On the 1st of this month, by the same [Rev. F. W. Kremer], Capt. P. Fischer, with Miss Anna M. Gerhart, both of this city [Lebanon].
On the 25th of December, by the Rev. A. Romich, Albert Hain with Mary Seltzer, both of Mt. Nebo.
On the 15th of January, by the same, Joseph F. Sarge, with Miss Anna Maria Bickel, both of Jonestown.
On the 29th, by the same [Rev. A. Romich], Jacob Umberger, with Miss Rebecca Yeagley, both of Swatara.

February 13, 1857

Married. On the 3rd of this month, by the Rev. H. S. Miller, Mr. David Bruch, of North Lebanon, with Elisabeth Fornwalt, of Cornwall.
On the 8th of this month, by the same [Rev. H. S. Miller], Charles Trimble, with ARabella Baltimore, both of this city [Lebanon].
On the 5th of this month, by the Rev. F. W. Kremer, Casper Scherk, with Susan Mc Connel, both of Lebanon.
On the 5th of this month, by the Rev. Aug. C. Wedekind, John A. Boyer, of Duncannaon, with Anna M. Groff, of the city of Lebanon.

February 20, 1857

Married. On the 12th of this month, by the Rev. F. W. Kremer, John H. Fortney, with Sarah Ann Emerich, both of North Lebanon Township.
On the 12th of this month, by the Rev. Aug. Wedekind, David Lang, with Civilla Schoop, both of Union Deposit, Dauphin County.
On the day named [February 12], by the same [Rev. Aug. C. Wedekind], David Landis, of Union Deposit, with Elizabeth Ann Miller, of North Annville.
On the 25th of December, by the Rev. Mr. Romich, Albert A. Hean, with Miss Mary C. Hoke, both of Mt. Nebo.

February 27, 1857

Married. On the 25th of December, by the Rev. J. E. Hiester, Mr. William Miller of Londonderry with Miss Mary Christ of South Annville.
On the 12th of January, by the same [Rev. J. E. Hiester], Mr. John Dutweiler, of South Annville, with Miss Mary Evy, of Conestoga, Lancaster County.

Der Libanon Demokrat                    Lebanon, Pa.

February 27, 1857 Continued

Married. On the 5th of this month, by the same [Rev. J. E. Hiester], Mr. Conrad Horstich, with Polly Deininger, both of Palmyra.
 On the same day [February 5], by the same [Rev. J. E. Hiester], Mr. Jacob Nitrauer, of Campbelltown, with Miss Sara Anna Ries, of Manadaville, Dauphin County.
 On the 17th of this month, by the same [Rev. J. E. Hiester], Mr. Christian Meyer, of Harrisburg, with Miss Rebecca Zimmerman, of Annville.
 On the 22nd of this month, by the Rev. J. S. Cook, Levi Hoffa, of Fredericksburg, with Helen E. Wilson, of Cumberland County.

March 6, 1857

Married. On the 26th of February, by the Rev. J. S. Cook, P. B. Misch, M. D., of Cornwall, this county, with Miss E. Catharine, daughter of the late General R. H. Hammond, of Milton, Pa.
 On the day named [February 26], by the same [Rev. J. S. Cook], Mr. John White, with Miss Anna Rodearmal, both of North Lebannon.
 On last Sunday evening [March 1], at the Uhler Hotel, by the Rev. Aug. C. Wedekind, Aaron Yocum with Miss Kate M. Heffner, both of Sinking Springs.
 On the 15th of February, by the Rev. Samuel Yingling, Mr. William L. Fischer, with Miss Mary Garberich, both of East Hanover Township.
 On the 22nd of February, by the same [Rev. Samuel Yingling], George Redsecker, of Conewago, Dauphin County, with Miss Anna E. Clendenin, of Londonderry Township.

March 13, 1857

Married. On the 22nd of January, by the Rev. Thos. H. Leinbach, Mr. William Strohm, with Miss Lydia Williams, both of Heidelberg Township.
 On the 29th, Mr. John Kessler, of Heidelberg Township, with Miss Catharina Ann Mell, of Richland, Berks County.
 On the 3rd of February, Mr. Isaac Gerhart, of Bethel Township, Lebanon County, with Miss Susanna Bensing, of Bethel Township, Berks County.
 On the 28th, Mr. Jacob Albert, of Bethel Township, with Miss Carolina Malvern, of Jackson Township, Lebanon County.
 On the 5th of this month, Mr. Michael Zeller, with Miss Amilia Weitzel, both of Heidelberg, Berks County.
 Likewise: Mr. Jacob Reifein, with Mrs. Catharina Daub, both of North Lebanon.

Der Libanon Demokrat                              Lebanon, Pa.

March 13, 1857 Continued

Married. On the 26th of February, by the Rev. C. F. McCauley, Mr. Thomas A. Harper, of East Hanover Township, with Miss Emma Warren of Reading.

On the 5th of this month, by the Rev. Michael Gingerich, Isaac Gingerich, of North Annville, with Miss Elisabeth Westenberger, of South Annville.

On the 22nd of February, by the Rev. Mr. Siegrist, Jacob Haughky, with Miss Lydia Ditzler, both of Clay Township, Lancaster County.

On the 24th, by the same [Rev. Siegrist], Mr. Aaron Baer, of Clay Township, with Miss Elisabeth Keath, of Elisabeth Township, Lancaster County.

On the 5th of this month, by the Rev. F. W. Kremer, Edmund T. Boltz, of North Annville, with Miss Rebecca Krall, of Swatara Township.

On the 5th of March, by the Rev. L. G. Eggers, William Batdorf, with Sarah Mordock, both of Jackson Township.

March 20, 1857

Married. On the 12th of this month, David Gingrich, of South Annville township, with Elisabeth Xander, of Londonderry Township.

On the 15th of February, by the Rev. Mr. Petri, Francis Hoffman, with Louisa Mengel, both of the city of Reading.

On the 8th of March, by the same [Rev. Petri], Josuah Kessler, with Catharina Gehres, both of Schuylkill County.

On the 5th of this month, by the Rev. John Stein, Henry Stichler, with Elizabeth Anspach, both of Hanover.

On the 26th of February, by the Rev. J. E. Hiester, Samuel Eckert, of North Annville, with Mary Ann Boltz, of Belleview [Bellegrove].

On the 5th of this month, by the same [Rev. J. E. Hiester], Thomas Boger, with Isabella A. Lebo, both of Belleview [Bellegrove].

March 27, 1857

Married. On the 19th of this month, by the Rev. C. S. Haman, John Smith, with Angeline Donmoyer, both of the city of Lebanon.

On the 11th of this month, by the Rev. Charles A. Hays, David B. Gingerich, of South Annville Township, with Elisabeth Sanders, only daughter of Johann Sanders, of Londonderry Township.

On the 19th of this month, by the Rev. J. S. Cook, John Sauers, of this city, with Catharine Uhler, of Lebanon.

Der Libanon Demokrat                          Lebanon, Pa.

March 27, 1857 Continued

Married. On the 23rd, by A. S. Ely, Esq, Lawrence Sander, with Mary Kurtz, both of Millcreek Township.
Some time ago, by the Rev. Mr. Eggers, Mr. William Batdorf, with Sarah Murdock, both of Jackson Township.

April 3, 1857

Married. On the 15th, by the Rev. Mr. Petri, John Gottschall, of Reading, with Miss Elmina Schwoyer, of Lehigh County.
On the 28th of the preceeding month, by J. Gelim, Esq., Henry Wolf, of North Lebanon Borough, with Catharina Speck, of Jackson Township.
On the 29th of the preceeding month, by the Rev. H. S. Miller, Alexander McGowan, of Harrisburg, with Amanda, daughter of Samuel Harbeson, of this city [Lebanon].

April 10, 1857

Married. On the 26th of March, by the Rev. F.Krecker, Mr. Samuel Ney, with Miss Regina Ney, both of Myerstown.
On the 2nd of this month, by the Rev. C. S. Haman, Mr. William F. Kreitz, of Myerstown, with Sarah L. Bossler, of Jackson.
On the 29th of March, by the Rev. John Stein, David Hassler, with Sabina Kreiser, both of Union Township. - On the 29th, Elias Wohlleder, with Ester Braunmiller, both of Bethel Township.

April 24, 1857

Married. On the 10th of April, by the Rev. J. Stein, Mr. Philip Braun, with Catharina Schmeltzer, both of Bethel Township, Berks County.
On Thursday, the 19th of this month, by the Rev. Mr. Rupp, Mr. Christian Guth, of Highspire, Dauphin County, with the widow of the late John Schneider, of Swatara, Lebanon County.

May 8, 1857

Married. On the 26th of April, by the Rev. Mr. Miller, George P. G. Smith, with Sarah Ann Jung, both of this city [Lebanon].
On the 5th of this month, by the Rev. F. W. Kremer, Edward R. Zimmerman, of East Hanover, with Miss Kate, daughter of Joseph Bomberger, of South Lebanon.

Der Libanon Demokrat					Lebanon, Pa.

### May 15, 1857

Married. On the 26th of last April, by the Rev. D. Hoffman, Mr. Andreas Nase [Nace], with Miss Ester Klein, both of North Lebanon Township.

On the 7th of this month, by the Rev. L. Klein, Mr. Jacob Hunsicker, with Miss Lydia Philbi, both of Lebanon County.

On the 7th of this month, by the Rev. A. C. Wedekind, Mr. John M. Faber, with Miss Lucetta C. Alleman, both of this city.

### May 22, 1857

Married. On the 7th of this month, by the Rev. Mr. Hoffman, Franklin Hambleton, with Miss Mary Zimmerman, both of Cornwall Township.

On the 12 of April, by the Rev. T. H. Leinbach, Dr. Griffith H. Scholl, of Segersville [Saegersville], Lehigh County, with Miss Angelina C. Salen, music teacher in Womelsdorf, Berks County.

On the 9th of this month, by the same [Rev. T. H. Leinbach], Daniel Wolf, with Miss Magdalena Bricker, both of Jackson.

On the 14th, by the same [Rev. T. H. Leinbach], Mr. John Seiders, of Schaefferstown, with Mary Ann Theis, of Jackson.

On the 16th of this month, by the same [Rev. T. H. Leinbach], Mr. John Helder, with Miss Eliza Ann Preis, both from nearby Womelsdorf, Berks County.

On the 17th, by the same [Rev. T. H. Leinbach], Mr. Solomon Matthew, with Miss Rebecca Bechtold, both of Marion, Berks County. - Likewise, Jacob H. Mace, with Miss Catharina Geiss, both of Newmanstown, LebanonCounty.

### May 29, 1857

Married. On the 19th of this month, by the Rev. John Stein, David Hetrich, with Miss Caroline Dotter, both of Hanover, Lebanon County.

On the 14th of this month, by the Rev. H. S. Miller, Henry Foltz, of Londonderry Township, with Miss Catharina Kreider, of Cornwall Township.

On the 20th of April, by the Rev. Samuel B. Becker, Jacob C. Licht [Light], formerly of Lebanon, with Miss Margaret Flitsch, both of New Boston, Illinois.

On the 14th of this month, by the Rev. J. J. Strine, John L. Epler, of South Annville, Lebanon County, with Miss Sarah Erb, of Warwick Township, Lancaster County.

On the 9th of December, by the Rev. Father McClaskey, Thomas H. Russell, of this city [Lebanon], with Mrs. Mary Reily of Philadelphia.

Der Libanon Demokrat                           Lebanon, Pa.

June 5, 1857

Married. On the 28th of May, by the Rev. John Stein, Adam Rittel, with Anna Meier, both of Bethel Township.
On the 31st of May, by the same [Rev. John Stein], Dewilla Donmeier, of Union Township, with Matilda Ely, of the city of Lebanon.

June 12, 1857

Married. On the 7th of this month, by the Rev. F. W. Kremer, Reuben Fessler, with Miss Lydia A. Yingst, both of North Lebanon Township.
On the 24th of May, by the Rev. Mr. Gring, John B. Schuey, of Union Township, with Miss Essie Boger, of South Annville.

June 19, 1857

Married. On the 11th of this month, by the Rev. F. W. Kremer, Peter Gerret, with Miss Rosanna Stover, both of Cornwall Township.
On the day named [June 11], by the same [Rev. F. W. Kremer], Mr. Jacob Becker, with Miss Ellen Seiders, both of Schaefferstown.
On the day named [June 11], by the same [Rev. F. W. Kremer], Adam Derkes, with Susan Schnebely, both of this city [Lebanon].

June 26, 1857

Married. On the 13th of this month, by the Rev. Mr. Stein, Mr. Heinrich Batdorf, with Miss Catharina Christ, both of Jackson Township, Lebanon County.
On the 21st, by the same, Mr. Peter Bucher, with Miss Catharina Walmer, both of Union Township, Lebanon County.
On the 18th of this month, by the Rev. H. S. Miller, Andrew Heintzelman, with Lucetta Kintzel, both of this city [Lebanon].
On the 21st of this month, by the Rev. F. W. Kremer, Jonas Geib, with Miss Catharina Eby, both of South Lebanon Township.
On the 4th of this month, by the Rev. A. Romich, Mr. Solomon Haak, of Swatara, with Catharina Schaud, of Jonestown.

July 3, 1857

Married. On the 28th of June, by the Rev. F. W. Kremer, Mr. George W. Mellinger, of this city [Lebanon], with Miss Eliza Lowry, of North Lebanon.

Der Libanon Demokrat                    Lebanon, Pa.
             July 3, 1857 Continued

Married. On the 20th of June, by the Rev. Mr. Gring, Mr. Henry Dollum, with Sarah Eberly, both of Jackson Township.

                July 10, 1857

Married. On the 5th of this month, by the Rev. H. S. Miller, Mr. John Scheetz, with Miss Matilda Wolf, both of Lebanon.
   On the 20th of June, by the Rev. Mr. Gring, Mr. Henry Dollum, with Sarah Eberly, both of Jackson Township.
   On the 2nd of this month, by the Rev. J. Y. Ashton, Mr. Benjamin Steffy, with Miss Anna Seider, both of Lebanon County.

                July 17, 1857

Married. On the 11th of July, 1857, by the Rev. Mr. Kleinfelter, Mr. Levi McFearling, of North Lebanon, with Miss Eliza Spaeth, of Millcreek.
   On the 7th of this month, by the Rev. Mr. Kremer, Mr. George F. Ely, of North Lebanon, with Miss Kate Fellenbaum, both of Lebanon.

                July 24, 1857

Married. On the 14th of this month, by Emanuel B. Salen, Esq, Mr. Samuel Lehman (widower), with Miss Polly Buffington (widow), both of East Hanover, Dauphin County.

                July 31, 1857

Married. On the 12th of July, by the Rev. Mr. Stein, Mr. Josua Boeshore, of Union Township, with Miss Maria Anna Gamber, of Swatara Township.
   On the 19th of this month, by the same [Rev. Stein], Mr. Andreas Gretscher, of Jonestown, with Miss Maria Bausman, of Hanover.
   On the 26th of this month, in Reading, by the Rev. C. S. Haman, John H. Schellenberger, of the city of Lebanon, with Miss Anna Mary Long, of Cornwall Township.

                August 7, 1857

Married. On the 12th of July, by the Rev. J. E. Hiester, Mr. John Rudy, with Miss SArah Anna Alt, both of Annville.

                August 14, 1857

Married. On the 28th of July, by the Rev. Mr. Schropp,

Der Libanon Demokrat                           Lebanon, Pa.

August 14, 1857 Continued

Mr. Christian W. Singel, with Miss Elizabeth L. Adams, both of Baltimore.
On the 6th of this month, by the Rev. Aug. C. Wedekind, Mr. James Yocum, of North Lebanon, with Miss Sarah Licht, of South Lebanon.
On the 9th of this month, by the same [Rev. Aug. C. Wedekind], Mr. Franklin G. Bemenderfer, with Miss Amanda H. Murdock, both of Schaefferstown.
On the 5th of this month, by the Rev. H. S. Miller, Mr. David Hughes, of Robesonia, with Miss Angelina Zweitzig, of Lebanon County.

August 21, 1857

Married. On the 18th of this month, by the Rev. Aug. C. Wedekind, Abraham Brechbill, with Miss Mary A. Kreider, both of South Lebanon Township.
On the 11th of this month, by the Rev. F. W. Kremer, Mr. George Steins, of Lebanon, with Miss Elisabeth Spangler, of Jackson Township.
On the 26th of July, by the Rev. John Stein, Mr. Washington Horn with Rebecca Helm, both of Jonestown. - On the 8th of this month, by the same [Rev. John Stein], John Henry Boeshore, with Lydianna Weiss, both of Union Township.

August 28, 1857

Married. On the 23rd of August, by the Rev. F. Krecher, Mr. Frnklin Siegrist, of Lancaster County, with Miss Leah Kleinfelter, of Lebanon County.
On the 12th of July, by the Rev. Mr. Siegrist, Levi Fetter, with Lovina Mattes, both of Heidelberg, Lebanon County.
On the 9th of August, by the same [Rev. Siegrist], Isaac Stie__, with Catharina Buchter, both of Clay Township, Lancaster County.
On the 20th of August, by the Rev. Mr. J. Stein, William H. Groh, of Berrysburg, Dauphin County, with Elizabeth Stein, of Hanover, Dauphin County.
On the 22nd, by the same [Rev. J. Stein], Johannes Fuchs [Fox], with Lea Ulrich, both of Bethel Township, Lebanon County.
On the 23rd, by the same [Rev. J. Stein], Heinrich Wiegand, with Catharina Miess, both of Union Township.
On the 25th, by the same [Rev. J. Stein], Johannes L. Saylor, of Annville Township, with Ellen Johanna Freylinghaus, of Jonestown, Lebanon County.

Der Libanon Demokrat　　　　　　　Lebanon, Pa.

### September 4, 1857

Married. On the 30th of August, by the Rev. Mr. Kremer, Mr. Levi A. Kreider, with Miss Susan C. Strohm, both of this city [Lebanon].

On the 27th, by the Rev. Mr. Wedekind, Mr. John Miller, with Eliza Zeller, both of North Lebanon Township.

### September 11, 1857

Married. By the Rev. Thos. H. Leinbach

On the 2nd of August, Mr. Cyrus Coller, with Miss Lucy Levengood, both of Tulpehocken, Berks County.

On the 18th, Jacob Schuhmacher, of Jackson, with Miss Louisa Wolf, of Millcreek.

On the 20th, Mr. Irael Bomberger, with Miss Leah Schmidt, both of Lebanon County.

On the 25th, Henry Zeller, of Millcreek, with Miss Sophia Haagte, of Lancaster County.

On the 27th, Percivell Zerbe, with Miss Carolina Schrieber, both of Newmanstown, Lebanon County.

On the 3rd of this month, George Himmelberger, with Mrs. Sarah R. Person, of Marion, both of Berks County.

On the 5th of this month, Henry Lutz, with Miss Malinda Daub, both of Lebanon County.

On the 3rd of this month, by the Rev. Aug. C. Wedekind, Mr. John Ettendyer, with Miss Mary Ann Hollinger, both of Dauphin County.

On the 1st of this month, by the Rev. F. W. Kremer, Mr. John Herchelroth, with Miss Catharina Fink, both of Cornwall Township.

On the 3rd of this month, by the same, Samuel Rager, with Miss Catharina Uhrich, both of Dauphin County.

By the Rev. H. S. Miller, John Hirchle [Hershley], with Angelius Hauscht, both of North Lebanon.

On the 3rd of this month, by the Rev. Fred. Krecker, Mr. Christian S. Braun, with Miss Eliza Evans, both of Lancaster County.

### September 18, 1857

Married. On the 14th of August, by the Rev. J. E. Hiester, Joseph Lessley, of Annville, with Miss Catharina Rank, of Belleview.

On the 15th of this month, by the Rev. F. W. Kremer, Simon Schnebely, with Miss Veronica Schnebely, both of Cornwall Township.

On the 5th of August, by the Rev. J. F. Brobst, Mr. John P. Gerhard, with Miss Amanda E. Lowry, both of the city of Lebanon.

Der Libanon Demokrat                     Lebanon, Pa.
                    September 25, 1857

Married. On the 17th of this month, by the Rev. T. Wunderling, Mr. Charles Stump, with Miss Carolina Miller, both of Lebanon.
   On the 17th of this month, by the Rev. F. W. Kremer, John H Uhler, with Miss Kate Kitzmiller, both of this city [Lebanon].

                    October 9, 1857

Married. On the 15th of September, by the Rev. T. H. Leinbach, Mr. John Heinege, with Miss Susanna Gackley, both of Lancaster County.
   On the 1st of this month, by the same [Rev. T. H. Leinbach], Mr. Edward Pfeifer, of Jackson Township, with Miss Carolina Behny, of Tulpehocken. - Likewise, Jonathan Seibert, with Susanna Winter, both of Tulpehocken. - Likewise, Cyrus Lerch, with Sarah Harner, both of Bethel, all of Berks County.
   On the 4th of this month, by the Rev. F. W. Kremer, Mr. Jacob Eckert, of North Lebanon, with Miss Harriet Stout, of this city [Lebanon].
   On the 6th of this month, by the same [Rev. F. W. Kremer], Mr. Joel Brubacher, of South Lebanon, with Catharina Kreider, of Cornwall Township.
   On the 1st of this month, by the Rev. Aug. C. Wedekind, Samuel S. Huntsberger, with Miss Anna B. Longenecker, both of Dauphin County.
   On the day named, by the same, Peter M. Cramer, with Miss Magdalena S. Longenecker, both of Dauphin County.

                    October 16, 1857

Married. On the 8th of this month, by the Rev. H. S. Miller, Mr. Anthony Gerhard, with Miss Sarah Ellenberger, both of this city [Lebanon].
   On the 24th of September, in Reading, by the Rev. L. Leinbach, Mr. Isaac Hain, of North Lebanon, with Miss Mary Ann Billman, of this city [Lebanon].
   On the 6th of this month, by the Rev. Samuel Yingling, Mr. John Stophel, of Derry, DAuphin County, with Mrs. Susannah Brown, of Londonderry, Lebanon County.
   On the 20th of September, by the Rev. Mr. Hoffman, Mr. Michael Clark, with Mrs. Mary A. Kuhns, both of Lebanon.
   On Tuesday, the 14th day, by the Rev. Mr. Hertzler, Moses Gippel, of Bethel, with Leah Wenger, of Swatara Township.
   On the 8th of this month, by the Rev. Mr. Hess, Mr. Henry Kissinger, of Heidelberg Township, with Miss Sarah Schuhmacher, of Heidelberg Township.

Der Libanon Demokrat                    Lebanon, Pa.

October 16, 1857 Continued

Married. On the 15th of June, by the Rev. Mr. Eggers, Thomas Heckman, of Heidelberg, with Catharina Barry, of Millcreek Township.
On the 22nd of September, by the Rev. C. Siegrist, John Getz, of Lebanon County, with Miss Rose Peter, of New York.
On the 1st of October, by the same [Rev. C. Siegrist], George Ruth, with Susannah Lynch, both of Clay Township, Lancaster County.

October 23, 1857

Married. On the 16th of this month, by the Rev. John Stein, Moses Scherk, of North Annville Township, with Miss Maria Magdalena Kohr, of Bethel Township.
On the 10th, by the same [Rev. John Stein], Mr. George Glick, of Jackson Township, with Miss Maria Anna Yoder, of North Lebanon Township.
On the 13th of this month, by the Rev. H. S. Miller, Mr. Jacob M. Smith, of Freeport, Illinois, with Miss Sarah Ann Shugar, of this city [Lebanon].
On the 15th of this month, by the Rev. F. W. Kremer, Mr. Henry D. Benson, with Miss Louisa Schaffer, both of Londonderry Township, Lebanon County.
On the 15th of this month, in Lancaster, by the Rev. Mr. Strine, Mr. William S. Ingham, with Miss Mary Arenz, both of Myerstown.

October 30, 1857

Married. On the 22nd of this month, by the Rev. H. S. Miller, Eliphas W. Stuckey, of Hanover, with Miss Catharina Anna Seiders, of Londonderry.
On the 20th of this month, by the Rev. T. H. Robinson, respected John C. Kunkel and Miss Elizabeth C. Rutherford, daughter of Dr. W. W. Rutherford, of Harrisburg.
On the 18th of this month, by the Rev. John Gring, Dr. R. H. Muth, formerly of Rehrersburg, Berks County, with Miss Maggie daughter of Isaac Hower, of Fredericksburg.
On last Sunday [October 18], by the Rev. Mr. Wolle, at Lititz, Mr. John Henry Oswald, of this city [Lebanon], with Miss Mary Amberg, of South Lebanon Township.

November 6, 1857

Married. By the Rev. Thos. H. Leinbach.
On the 8th of October, Franklin Wenrich, with Miss Sarah Klopp, both of Stouchsburg, Berks County.

Der Libanon Demokrat                    Lebanon, Pa.

             November 6, 1857 Continued

Married. On the 11th of October, David Moyer, with Miss Caroline Weigley, both of Millcreek Township.
   On the 18th of October, Henry Moore, with Mrs. Elisabeth Kiener, of Schaefferstown.
   On the 31st of October, John Lutz, with Miss Lavina Heck, both of Berks County.
   On the 18th of this month, by the Rev. Mr. Gring, Dr. R. H. Muth, formerly of Rehrersburg, with Maggie, daughter of Isaac Hauer, of Fredericksburg.
   On the 19th of October, by Joseph Cooper, Esq., John Wagner, with Miss Amanda Helder, both of Jackson Township.
   On the 22nd of October, by C. P. Miller, Esq., Mr. Jacob Xander, of East Hanover Township, with Miss Mary Koons, of Union Township.
   On the 20th of August, by the Rev. J. Y. Ashton, Daniel McKinney, with Ann Miller, both of North Lebanon.
   On the 1st of September, by the same [Rev. J. Y. Ashton], Samuel Scheiner, with Miss Susan Hornefius, both of North Lebanon.
   On the 29th of September, by the same, [Rev. J. Y. Ashton], John E. Smith, with Miss Catharina Kiscadden, both of Cornwall Township.
   On the 29th of October, by the Rev. F. W. Kremer, John A. Bauman, of Cornwall Township, with Miss Mary Hoffer, of South Annville Township.
   By H, S. Miller, John H. Fritz, with Miss Malinda Burkhart, both of Rehrersburg.
   By the same [Rev. H. S. Miller], Absalom Webber of Schuylkill Haven, with Mrs. Susan M. Stoever, of Lebanon.

                November 13, 1857

Married. On the 5th of November, by the Rev. Friedrich Krecker, Mr. Cyrus Wolf, with Miss Elisabeth Noll, both of Myerstown.
   By the Rev. John Stein.
   On the 29th of October, Jacob Heilman, with Maria Braun, both of Jonestown.
   On the 1st of this month, Reuben L. Seasholtz, with Sarah Spangler, both of Myerstown.
   On the 8th of this month, Allen Weigley, of Myerstown, with Anna Elisabeth English, of Jonestown.
   On the 5th of this month, by the Rev. Aug. C. Wedekind, Allen W. Mentzer, of Lancaster County, with Miss Fianna Dibbel, of Millcreek Township.

Der Libanon Demokrat                    Lebanon, Pa.
November 20, 1857

Married. By the Rev. Johannes Stein.
On the 12th of this month, Samuel Hautz, with Rebecca Gundrum, both of Bethel Township.
On the day named [November 12], Joseph Miller, with Lea Deck, both of East Hanover Township.
For several weeks, by the Rev. Jacob Reinhold, Mr. David Zug, of Heidelberg Township, with Miss Elisabeth Moyer, of Bethel Township, Berks County.
On the 29th of October, by the Rev. J. E. Hiester, Mr. Joseph Kreider, of South Annville Township, with Miss Leah Moyer, of North Annville Township.
On the 5th of this month, by the same [Rev. J. E. Hiester], John Nye, of Palmyra, with Mary E. Wolfersberger, of Derry Township, Dauphin County.
On the 12th of this month, by the same [Rev. J. E. Hiester], Mr. John H. Wolfersberger, of Campbelltown, with Miss Catharina Bachman, of South Annville Township.
On the day named [November 12], by the same [Rev. J. E. Hiester], Peter Pickel, of South Annville Township, with Miss Elisabeth Becker, of Lancaster County.

November 27, 1857

Married. On the 18th of October, by the Rev. D. Moyers, William Scheiner, of Lebanon, with Sarah Miller, of Myerstown.
On the 24th by the same [Rev. D. Moyers], William Ochs, of Myerstown, with Emilie Kelchner, of Jackson Township. On the 31st, by the same [Rev. D. Moyers], Mr. Peter Brubacher, of Schaefferstown, with Catharina Behny, of Myerstown.
On the 24th of this month, by C. S. Haman, Mr. Elias Marks, with Rebecca Nagel, both of the city of Lebanon.
On the 29th of October, by the Rev. J. E. Hiester, Mr. Joseph Kreider, of South Annville, with Miss Lea Moyer, of North Annville.
On the 5th of this month, by the same [Rev. J. E. Hiester], Mr. John Ney, of Palmyra, with Miss Mary E. Wolfersberger, of Derry Township, Dauphin County.
On the 12th of this month, by the same [Rev. J. E. Hiester], Mr. John Henry Wolfersberger, of Campbelltown, with Miss Catharina Bachman, of South Annville.
On the 19th of this month, by the same [Rev. J. E. Hiester], Mr. Joseph Horst, with Miss Anna Rudy, both of Londonderry.
On the 24th of this month, by the same [Rev. J. E. Hiester], Mr. John Henry, with Miss Jane Eliza Mark, both of Belleview [Bellegrove].

Der Libanon Demokrat				Lebanon, Pa.

December 4, 1857

Married. On the 26th of November, by the Rev. T. H. Leinbach, Mr. Jacob Edris, with Miss Catharina Ann Scherk, both of Jackson Township, Lebanon County.
On the 21st, by the same [Rev. T. H. Leinbach], Mr. Daniel Klar, with Miss Catharina Lengel, both of Bethel. Likewise, Mr. John Reber, with Miss Catharina Strauss. both of near Bernville, all of Berks County.
On the 26th of November, by the Rev. Aug. C. Wedekind, Charles Benson, of North Lebanon, with Sarah Hauck, of Jackson Township.
On the day named [November 26], by the same [Rev. Aug. C. Wedekind], Jos. Witman, of Derry Township, Dauphin County, with Mary Stehley, of West Hanover, Dauphin County.
On the day named [November 26], by the same [Rev. Aug. C. Wedekind], Henry Hegy, with Leah Sahm, both of Penn Township, Lancaster County.
On the 24th of November, by the Rev. F. W. Kremer, Isaac Brandt, of North Lebanon Township, with Rosanna Dubbs, of this city [Lebanon].
On the 26th, by the same [Rev. Aug. C. Wedekind], William Bleistein, of North Lebanon Township, with Elisabeth Jacoby, of Jackson Township.
On the day named [November 26], by the same [Rev. Aug. C. Wedekind], Mr. Philip Schaak, with Miss Catharina Schmidt, both of South Lebanon Township.
On the 26th, by the Rev. H. S. Miller, John Schimp, with Miss Eliza Metz, of Cornwall.
On the day named [November 26], by the same [Rev. H. S. Miller], Kelumban Schreiber, with Anna Kuntzelman, of Lebanon.
On the 29th, by the Rev. John Stein, Josiah H. Rank, with Amelia Heilman, both of Jonestown.
On the 26th, by the Rev. A. S. Leinbach, George R. Eckert, Esq., of Reading, with Rebecca Gerhard, of Millcreek Township.

December 11, 1857

Married. On the 3rd of November, by the Rev. Samuel Yingling, John Kinsey, of Dauphin County, with Miss Magdalena Hess, of Londonderry Township, Lebanon County.
On the 15th, by the same, Samuel Forney, with Rosanna Radabach, both of Palmyra.
On the 26th, by the Rev. Lewis G. Eggers, John H. Steiner, with Sara Ann Lehman, both of Jackson Township.
On the 26th, by the same, William E. Brunner, of Jonestown, with Miss Louisa Hacker, of Campbelltown.
On the 27th, by Solomon Schmidt, Esq., Daniel Brandt, with Miss Elisabeth Gerret, both of North Lebanon Borough.

Der Libanon Demokrat                    Lebanon, Pa.
            December 11, 1857 Continued

Married. On the 26th, by the Rev. N. S. Strassburger, Jacob G. Gabel, of Lebanon, with Miss Mary Ann Stauffer, of Boyertown, Berks County.
   On the day named, by the Rev. C. A. Hay, Samuel S. Groff, of Lancaster County, with Miss Elisabeth Reinhard, of Lebanon County.
   On the day named, by the same [Rev. C. A. Hay], George Biemesderfer, of Lancaster County with Miss Catharina Kiener, of Lebanon County.
   On the 1st of this month, by the Rev. Aug. C. Wedekind, Chambers Bobb, of Schaefferstown, with Miss Mary Seibert, of Millcreek.
   On the 1st of this month, by the Rev. F. W. Kremer, William B. Kreider, with Elisabeth Witmer, both of Cornwall Township.
   On the 3rd, by the same [Rev. F. W. Kremer], Edward Backenstose, of East Hanover, with Nancy Landis, of Derry Township, Dauphin County.
   On the 1st, by the Rev. Charles A. Hay, Hiram Siegrist, of Lebanon County, with Mary Schnebely, of Baltimore County, Md.

                December 18, 1857

Married. On the 3rd of this month, by the Rev. Mr. Stein, Johannes Bolton, with Maria Schuey, both of Dauphin County.
   On the day named [December 3], by the same [Rev. Stein], Wilhelm Behler, with Sara Ann Gassert, both of North Lebanon.
   On the 10th of December, by the same [Rev. Stein], Wilhelm Wolf, with Maria Fassnacht, both of Bethel Township, Lebanon County.
   On the 10th of this month, by the Rev. F. W. Kremer, George Zerbe, of South Lebanon, with Catharina Philippy, both of Heidelberg Township.
   On the 10th, by the Rev. Aug. C. Wedekind, Christopher McGarveg, of Campbelltown, with Miss Anna M. Hall, of South Lebanon.
   On the day named, by the same, Henry Klein, with Miss Ellen Keller, both of South Hanover Township, Dauphin County.
   Some time ago, by the Rev. Hoffman, Mr. Benjamin Heilman, with Lea Theis, both of North Lebanon Township.

                December 25, 1857

Married. By the Rev. D. Hoffman.
   On the 26th of November, Daniel Weber, with Elisabeth Licht [Light], both of Lebanon.

Der Libanon Demokrat                       Lebanon, Pa.

December 25, 1857 Continued

Married. On the 1st of December, Abraham Herr, with Sarah Merk, both of North Annville.
On the 3rd, Henry Winter, with Angelina Seibert, both of East Hanover Township.
On the day named [December 3], George Hoffer, of South Annville, with Lydia Moyer, of North Annville.
On the 6th, Cyrus Merk, with Rebecca Strohm, both of Fredericksburg.
On the 19th of this month, by the Rev. C. Siegrist, Joseph Ried, with Catharina Price, both of Millcreek Township.
On the 17th of this month, by the Rev. F. W. Kremer, Cyrus Bleistein, of this city [Lebanon], with Miss Rosanna Fox, of South Lebanon Township.
On the 17th of this month, by the Rev. H. S. Miller, Friederich Dondeur, with Miss Dorothy Preusy, both of North Lebanon.
On the 17th of this month, by the Rev. Isaac Hess, John Kurtz, of Millcreek, with Julianna Kleinfelter, of Heidelberg Township.
On the 10th of this month, by the Rev. L. G. Eggers, Levi Geiser, with Rebecca Anthony, both of Myerstown, Lebanon County.
On the 17th, by the same [Rev. L. G. Eggers], Joseph Kindig, of South Lebanon Township, with Miss Polly Banage, of Cocalico, Lancaster County.
On the 15th of this month, by the Rev. J. F. Yeager, Dr. Lewis A. Lebenguth with Isabella, only daughter of Eli Filbert, both of Womelsdorf.

January 1, 1858

Married. On the 19th of November, by the Rev. Mr. Yeager, Aaron Weidman, with Nancy Keller, both of Ephrata, Lancaster County.
On the 1st of October, by the Rev. Mr. Steigerwalt, Abraham Baumgartner, of East Hanover Township, with Miss Elisabeth Fitting, of Dauphin County.
By the same [Rev. Steigerwalt], Mr. Daniel Gensemer, with Miss Catharin Loos, both of Lancaster County.
On the 22nd of December, by the same [Rev. Steigerwalt], Gideon Etter, of Lebanon County, with Miss Margaret Ann Brubacher, of Dauphin County.
By the Rev. A. Romig.
On the 8th of October, Daniel Krall, with Miss Elisabeth Batdorf. - On the 25th of October, William Boltz, with Elvina Hartman. - On the 20th of December, Peter Anspach, with Amelia Hartman, both of Union Township.

Der Libanoner                              Lebanon, Pa.

           January 1, 1858 Continued

Married. By the Rev. J. Stein.
     On the 17th of December, Jacob Fornwald, with Lusinda Kratzer, both of Londonderry Township.
     On the 22nd, the Rev. Abraham Romig, with Miss Sabina Elisabeth Stein, both of Jonestown.
     On the 24th of December, by the Rev. H. S. Miller, Peter Brenner, with Eliza Lantz, both of Dauphin County.
     On the day named [December 24], by the same [Rev. H. S. Miller], George W. Hoffman, with Lucy Ann Reidel, both of North Lebanon.
     On the 24th, by the Rev. Fred. Krecker, John W. Moyer, with Miss Maria E. Boyer, both of Myerstown.
     On the 24th, by the Rev. J. Stein, Jacob Kassel, with Miss Catharina Lantz, both of Union Township.
     On the 24th of December, by the Rev. J. E. Hiester, John W. Mann, of Londonderry Township, with Miss Sarah Lutz, of West Hanover Township, Dauphin County.
     On the day named [December 24], by the same [Rev. J. E. Hiester], Josia Fies, with Miss Sarah Batdorf, both of Cornwall.
     On the 1st of this month, by the same [Rev. J. E. Hiester], Daniel Kieser, with Miss Lea Zimmerman, both of West Hanover, Dauphin County.

                January 8, 1858

Married. On the 31st of December, by the Rev. Mr. Wedekind, Mr. John Bollack, of Cornwall, with Miss Louisa Bassler, of Mt. Joy.
     On the 29th, by the Rev. Mr. Miller, Mr. Samuel Bemesderfer, of North Lebanon, with Miss Ellen Louisa Sower, of Lebanon.
     On the 21st by the Rev. Mr. Kremer, Mr. John P. Hibschman, of Lancaster County, with Miss Sarah Yingst, of Lancaster County.

                January 15, 1858

Married. On the 24th of December, by the Rev. J. E. Hiester, John W. Mann, of Londonderry, with Sarah Lutz, of West Hanover, Dauphin County.
     On the day named, by the same [Rev. J. E. Hiester], Josiah Fies, with Sarah Batdorf, both of Cornwall.
     On the 7th of this month, by the Rev. H. S. Miller, Henry Kupp, with Fayette Fasnacht, both of North Annville.
     On the 9th of this month, by A. S. Ely, Esq., Henry Mies, with Mary Nine, both of East Hanover.

Der Libanon Demokrat　　　　　　　　　　Lebanon, Pa.

January 22, 1858

Married. On the 12th of this month, by the Rev. F. W. Kremer, John Fox, with Miss Ann Donley, both of North Lebanon.
On the 1st of January, by the Rev. John K. Kleinfelter, Joseph Hartman, with Miss Eva Laucks, of Millcreek, Lebanon County.

January 29, 1858

Married. On the 6th of December, by the Rev. Samuel Yingling, Henry Fischer, of Londonderry Township, with Miss Susan Herschey, of East Hanover.
On the 7th of this month, by the same [Rev. Samuel Yingling], David S. Elliot, of Hummelstown, with Miss Ann Caroline France, of Londonderry Township.
On the 21st of this month, by the Rev. A. C. Wedekind, John Field, of Union Deposit, with Miss Rebecca Fausler, of Londonderry Township.
On the day named [January 21], by the same [Rev. A. C. Wedekind], Lewis Fisch, with Miss Caroline Ehrman, both of Union Deposit.
On the 19th of this month, by the Rev. Thomas H. Leinbach, Mr. William Klopp, with Miss Sarah Ann Wenrich, both of Berks County.
On the 24th, by the same [Rev. Thomas H. Leinbach], Joseph Mattes, with Mrs. Redosia Philippi, both of Jackson Township.
On the day named [January 24], by the same [Rev. Thomas H. Leinbach], John H. Rittel, of North Lebanon Township, with Miss Lavina Spittler, of Bethel Township.
On the 21st of this month, by the Rev. F. W. Kremer, Henry Werner, D. S., of South Lebanon, with Mrs. Mary Schaak, of Jackson Township.
On the day named [January 21], by the same [Rev. F. W. Kremer], John H. Heisey, with Miss Catharina Schives, both of North Lebanon.

February 5, 1858

Married. On the 26th of November 1857, by the Rev. J. Y. Ashton, Mr. John Nagle, with Miss Leah Cunard, both of Colebrook, Lebanon County.
On the 28th of January, by the Rev. F. W. Kremer, Mr. Christian Snavely, with Miss Maria Snavely, both of South Annville.
On the 7th of January, by the Rev. Johannes Stein, John Wolf with Susanna Miller, both of Londonderry Township. - On the 23rd, Nathan Christ, of Jackson Township, with Susanna Uhrich, of Bethel Township. - On the 31st, Henry Roth, with Susanna Miller, both of Union Township.

Der Libanon Demokrat                              Lebanon, Pa.

February 12, 1858

Married. On the 4th of this month, by the Rev. Mr. Krecker, Mr. Samuel L. Fischer, of North Lebanon, with Miss Maria F. Derr, of Lebanon.
   On the 4th of this month, by the Rev. C. S. Haman, Jeremiah Boas, with Miss Catharina Womelsdorf, both of the city of Lebanon.
   On the 28th of January, in Lewistown, Pa., by the Rev. James S. Woods, D. D., Cyrus K. Merk, of Belleview City, Nebraska Territory, with Mrs. Mary Hoover, widow of the late Dr. L. Hoover, of Lewistown.

February 19, 1858

Married. On the 11th of this month, by the Rev. H. S. Miller, Solomon Boyer, of North Lebanon, with Miss Rebecca Ermel, of Swatara Township.

February 26, 1858

Married. On the 16th of this month, in Lancaster, by the Rev. G. F. Krotel, Tob. Reinoehl, publisher of the <u>Lebanon Courier</u>, with Miss Kate M. Ellinger, of Lancaster City.
   On the 7th of this month, in Connersville, Iowa, William W. Moyer, formerly of Fredericksburg, Lebanon County, with Miss Mary Eisenhauer, of Fayette County, Pa.

March 5, 1858

Married. On the 4th of January, by the Rev. Thos. H. Leinbach, Mr. John G. Moyer, with Miss Catharina Lamp, both of Tulpehocken. - On the 11th, by the same [Rev. Thos. H. Leinbach], William Gasser, of Bethel, with Miss Maria Riethy, of Marion, all of Berks County.
   On the 25th, by the same [Rev. Thos. H. Leinbach], Levi J. Groh, of Jackson, with Miss Anna Seltzer, of Myerstown.
   On the 25th of February, by the Rev. H. S. Miller, John Borry, with Elisabeth R. Trump, both of North Lebanon.

March 12, 1858

Married. On the 25th of February, by the Rev. J. E. Hiester, Mr. William Shetler, of East Hanover, with Miss Catharina Frantz, of Londonderry.
   On the 25th of February, by the same [Rev. J. E. Hiester], Mr. Joseph Dernhert, of Londonderry, with Miss Lea Runkel, of North Annville.

Der Libanon Demokrat                    Lebanon, Pa.

             March 12, 1858 Continued

Married. On the 2nd of this month, by the Rev. Samuel Miller, Jerome Haak, of Myerstown, with Miss Sarah Meiser, of Millcreek Township.
   By the Rev. John Stein.
   On the 6th of February, William Batdorff, with Amalia Sattazahn, both of Swatara Township.
   On the 27th, Emanuel Miller, with Eva Burkhart, both of Bethel Township.
   On the day named [February 27], John Rauch, with Catharina Rittel, both of Bethel Township.
   On the 7th of this month, by the Rev. F. W. Kremer, Henry Dohner, with Miss Mary Kreider, both of Cornwall Township.
   On the 13th of February, by the Rev. Lewis G. Eggers, Thomas Berger, of Clay, Lancaster County, with Sara Ibach, of Millcreek, Lebanon County.
   On the 4th of this month, by the same [Rev. Lewis G. Eggers], Henry Witman, with Sara Fox, both of Jackson, Township.

                March 19, 1858

Married. On the 14th of this month, by the Rev. A. S. Leinbach, William Lausch, of the city of Lebanon, with Emeline Lemmer, of Annville.

                March 26, 1858

Married. On the 11th of this month, by the Rev. Thomas H. Leinbach, Mr. Cyrus Dissinger, with Miss Catharina Yingst, both of Heidelberg Township.
   On the 18th, by the same [Rev. Thomas H. Leinbach], Mr. Richard Muth, with Mrs. Catharina Burkholder, both of Jackson Township, all of Lebanon County.
   On the 18th of this month, by the Rev. Fred Krecker, the Rev. C. S. Haman, recently of the city of Lebanon, with Miss Catharina Ann Reinoehl, of the same place.

                April 2, 1858

Married. On the 13th of March, by the Rev. Mr. Huber, Abraham Stager, F. S., formerly of Lebanon County, with Miss Rachel Rebert, both of Richland County, Ohio.
   On the 18th of March, by the Rev. A. C. Wedekind, Jacob Schwartz, of Lebanon, with Mrs. Susan Fox, of Campbelltown.
   On the 25th, by the same [Rev. A. C. Wedekind], Aaron Bricker, with Miss Mary Ann Boyer, both of North Lebanon Borough.
   On the 28th of March, by the Rev. F. W. Kremer,

Der Libanon Demokrat                                Lebanon, Pa.
             April 2, 1858 Continued

Henry Hornberger, with Miss Mary Dohner, both of Cornwall.
On the 18th, by the same [Rev. F. W. Kremer], Richard Muth, with Mrs. Catharina Burkholder, both of Jackson.

                 April 9, 1858

Married. On the 1st of this month, by the Rev. Jacob Reinhold, Mr. David Yingst, of Jackson township, with Miss Catharina Zug, of Heidelberg Township.
On the 24th of March, by A. S. Ely, Esq., Alois Kasper, with Miss Peterine Geiser, both of the city of Lebanon.

                April 16, 1858

Married. On the 4th of March, by the Rev. Johann Stein, Ruben Donmoyer, with Miss Lawina Kohr, both of Union Township. - On the 11th of March, Peter Dieben, with Sarah Kreiser, both of Union Township. - On the 4th of this month, William McGinley, of Annville Township, with Elisabeth Gerberich, of Hanover.
On the 10th of this month, by the Rev. H. S. Miller, George Gossert, of Lebanon, with Miss Susannah Kaufman, of North Lebanon.

                April 30, 1858

Married. On the 22nd of January, Lewis Donmeyer, with Miss Mary Hetz, both of Union Township.
On the 27th of March, by the same, Carl Meyer, with Miss Amanda Barto, both of Jonestown.
On the 17th of this month, by the Rev. Mr. Romich, George Walter, of Jonestown, with Miss Mary A. Gier, of Fredericksburg.
On the 21st, by the same [Rev. Romich], Daniel H. Eckert, with Miss Margaretta Rauch, both of East Hanover.
On the 20th, by the same [Rev. Romich], Peter Anspach, with Miss Amilia Hartman, both of Jonestown.
On the 15th of this month, by the Rev. Mr. Wedekind, William Lauden, with Miss Maria Greenblatt, both of Codorus, York County.
On the 18th, by the same [Rev. Wedekind], Mr. William R. Bentz, of Lebanon, with Rebecca L. Simenton, of Hummelstown.
On the day named [April 30], by the Rev. Mr. Miller, Samuel Gasser of Lebanon, with Catharina Dreist of Cornwall.
On the 15th of this month, by the Rev. J. Oswald, William S. Schay, Esq., publisher of the York Republican, with Miss Annie Upp, both of York.

Der Libanon Demokrat                    Lebanon, Pa.

April 30, 1858 Continued

Married. By the Rev. Mr. ___derling, Mr. Michael Felke, with Miss Catharina Kauffman, both of Cornwall Township.

May 20, 1859

Married. On the 17th of April, by the Rev. Mr. L. G. Eggers, Levi Kapp, of Newmanstown, with Miss Elisabeth Person, of Heidelberg, Berks County.
On the 8th of this month, by the Rev. R. Yeakel, John Berkeizer, with Miss Mary Dillman, both of Cornwall Township.
On the day named [May 8], by the Rev. J. Gross, John Faber with Mary Hautz, both of Fredericksburg.

May 10, 1860

Married. On the 15th of April, by the Rev. Johannes R. Kleinfelter, David Hartman with Lea Malm, both of Millcreek Township.
On the 6th of this month, by the Rev. J. E. Hiester, Ernst Bauerfreund with Carolina Beck, both of Annville, Lebanon County.
On the 15th of April, by the same [Rev. J. E. Hiester], William Thrash of Cornwall, with Rosanna Hoffert of South Lebanon.

August 29, 1861

Married. On the 19th of this month, in Johnstown, Cambria County, Albert Hartman, formerly of the city of Lebanon, with an attractive lady of that city.
On the 27th, by the Rev. Thomas H. Leinbach, Mr. Adam S. Riechard with Sophia Manbeck, both of Bernville, Berks County.
On the 10th of this month, by the same [Rev. Thomas H. Leinbach], Mr. William Werner, of Bethel, Lebanon County, with Maria Malleck, of Bethel, Berks County.
On the 22nd of this month, by the Rev. H. S. Miller, George Black, of North Lebanon Township, with Sarah Duppel of Jackson.
On the 25th of this month, by the same [Rev. H. S. Miller], Jonathan T. Werner, of Schuylkill Haven, with Eliza Donnenberger, of Jackson Township.
On the 18th of this month, by the Rev. William Gerhardt, Amos Diener with Mary Fischer, both of Union Township.
On the 18th of this month, by the Rev. A. Romig, John H. Black, with Elizabeth Wimberger, both of Annville.
On the 25th of this month, by the Rev. J. Stamm, J. H. Blouch with Lydia Sauden, both of North Lebanon.

Der Libanon Demokrat                              Lebanon, Pa.

August 29, 1861 Continued

Married. On the 25th of this month, by the Rev. J. E. Hiester, Henry Knoll with Louisa Boltz, both of North Annville.
On the 1st of this month, by the same [Rev. J. E. Hiester], Jerry Peffley with Jane Huy, both of East Hanover.

July 23, 1863

Married. On the 9th of July, by the Rev. J. E. Hiester, Mr. Henry Y. Urich, of North Annville, with Miss Elizabeth Clay, of East Hanover.
On the evening of the 16th of this month, in Philadelphia, by Mayor Henry, according to the ceremony of the Friends (Quakers), Louis Bowman with Sallie Taylor, both of Philadelphia.

April 7, 1864

Married. On the 3rd of this month, by the Rev. S. S. Chubb, John Scherk, with Mrs. Mary A. Weis, both of Cornwall.
On the 24th of March, by the Rev. G. P. Weaver, Daniel Ulrich, of Annville, with Ann Margaret Snavely, of Cornwall.

ADDENDA

Libanon County Demokrat                    Lebanon, Pa.

February 3, 1832

Married. On last sunday [January 29], by the Rev. Mr. Ernst, Mr. George Weirich, of Lebanon Township with Miss Sarah Spanhst, of Bethel Township.

On the day named [January 29], by the same gentleman [Rev. Ernst], Mr. Joseph Heilman with Miss Elisabeth Schnebely, both of Lebanon Township.

Also, by the same [Rev. Ernst], Mr. Joseph Boyer, with Miss Rebecca Fasnacht, both of Lebanon Township and all of Lebanon County.

INDEX

Aachenderfer, Samuel - 34
Achenbach, Catharina - 40
    Emeline - 54
    Hannah - 45
    Mary Ann - 9
Achey, Jeremias - 51
    John - 51
Ackerman, Catharina - 20
Adams, Elizabeth L. - 81
    George - 35
    Sophie - 73
Albert, Abraham - 71
    Jacob - 34, 75
    John - 48
    Joseph B. - 58
    Maria - 49
    Moses H. - 29
    Susanna - 57
Albrecht, Frederica - 68
Allbrecht, George - 18
Alleman, Henry - 20
    Lucetta C. - 78
    Mildred - 40
Allen, James L. - 68
Allison, John - 9, 10
Alt, Sarah Anna - 80
Altenderfer, William - 27
Amberg, Mary - 84
Anderson, Josiah - 72
Anspach, Catharina - 32
    Catharine - 4
    Elisabeth - 76
    Jonathan - 60
    Peter - 89, 94
Anthony, Rebecca - 89
Arenz, Mary - 84
Armstrong, Margaret Ann - 23
Arndt, John - 36
    Moses - 35
Arnold, John - 25
    Louisa - 2
Artz, Abraham - 25
    Catharina - 56
    Heinrich - 68
Atkins, John J. - 54
    Matilda M. - 32
    Susan - 22
    William - 32
Atlet, Annie - 9
Ault, Rebecca - 7
    William - 52
Auman, Benjamin - 53

Bachmaa, Catharina - 86 (2)
    Cyrus - 8
    Michael - 13
Backenstose, Edward - 88
Backholder, David - 39
Bader, Susanna - 23
Baddorf, L. - 69
Badorf, Elisabeth - 73
Baer, Aaron - 76
    George - 72
    Magdalina - 8
    Rebecca - 17
Baker, Catharina - 9
Baldwin, Ann - 42
Balm, Elisabeth - 61
Baltimore, Arabella - 74
Bamberger, Sarah - 56
Banage, Polly - 89
Bar, Carolina - 45
Bard, John - 52
Barry, Catharina - 84
Barto, Amanda - 94
Bartolet, Abraham - 18
Barton, Rosina - 52
Barwig, Elisabeth - 5
Bassler, Louisa - 90
Batdorf, Carolina - 48
    Elisabeth - 89
    Heinrich - 79
    Johannes - 33
    John - 51, 55
    Peter - 36
    Sarah - 90 (2)
    William - 76, 77
Batdorff, William - 93
Bates, Joseph B. - 52
Batz, Gideon - 55
Bauerfreund, Ernst - 95
Baum, Carolina Elisabeth - 26
Bauman, Barbara - 47
    Christopher - 18
    Elisabeth - 68
    Elisabetha - 51
    John A. - 85
    Mary A. - 49
    Moses L. - 21
Baumgartner, Abraham - 89
    Elisabeth - 23
    Slm. - 73
Bausman, Maria - 80
Beaumont, A. - 15
    Julia - 15

Bechtel, Christiana - 68
    Isaac - 51
    Michael - 4
    William - 50
Bechtold, John - 15
    Rebecca - 78
Beck, Carolina - 95
    Mack - 60
    Priscilla - 14
Becker, Catharina - 1
    Elisabeth - 86
    George - 8
    Jacob - 33, 79
    John - 8
    John L. - 8
    Rebecca - 63
    Sarah M. - 56
Beckley, Leah - 25
    Susanna - 51
Becky, Mary Ann - 53
Beeber, Joseph - 50
Behler, Wilhelm - 88
Behley, Priscilla - 73
Behm, Elisabeth - 21
Behny - 38
Behny, Carolina - 83
    Catharina - 86
    Elisabeth - 53
    Henry - 6
    Johannes - 72
    John -32
    Samuel - 22
    William - 6
Bell, Carolina - 50
    Samuel - 40
Bemenderfer, Franklin G. - 81
    William - 73
Bemerderfer, Cyrus - 40
Bemesderfer, Samuel - 90
Bender, Anna Maria - 46
    Carolina - 30
    Devilla - 22
    Eliza - 38
    Jacob - 36
    John - 35, 42
    Louisa - 18
    Mary Ann - 66
    Melinda - 20
    Reuben - 72
    Sarah - 47
    Tobias R. - 40
Bene, Louisa - 7
Benetch, Catharina - 26
Bennethum, Rebecca - 11
Bennethum, Susanna - 15
Bennetum, Catharina - 72
Bensing, Ellen - 68
    Peter - 10
    Susanna - 75
Benson, Catharina - 73
    Charles - 87
    Elisabeth - 4
    Henry D. - 84
    Johann - 4
    John - 71
Bentz, William R. - 94
Bergelbach, Elisabeth - 39
Berger, Thomas - 93
Bergner, Rebecca - 33
Berkheiser, Esther - 41
Berkeiser, John - 95
Berlot, Nathaniel - 57
Bernhart, Joseph - 92
Betz, Isaac - 18
    Samuel - 5
Bibee, Joseph - 23
Bicher, Benjamin - 64
    Sarah - 23
    William - 39
Bickel, Anna Maria - 74
    Samuel - 29
    Willemina - 29
Bicksler, Benjamin - 73
Bieber, Henry D. - 47
Biecher, Elizabeth - 69
    Samuel - 30
Biegeman, Foster - 15
Biemerderfer, Harriet - 32
    Rosianna - 65
Biemesderfer, George - 88
Biener, Susanna - 36
Biever, Saraḩ - 67
Billman, Mary Ann - 83
Binckley, Sarah - 65
Bingeman, Daniel - 20
Binner, Ann - 63
    Cyrus - 35
Bird, Adleine - 62
Bischop, Angelina - 7
    John - 7
    Reuben - 40
    William - 32
Bixler, John - 40
Black, Elisabeth - 46
    George - 95
    Hugh - 21
    John - 7
    John H. 95

Black, Sibilla - 22  
    William - 58  
Blatt, Rebecca -15  
Blauch, Gideon - 32  
    Lydia - 27  
    Nancy - 47  
    Rebecca - 52  
    William - 65  
Blecker, Sarah - 42  
Bleistein, Abraham - 73  
    Angelina - 8  
    Cyrus - 89  
    George - 42  
    Maria - 62  
    Samuel - 16  
    William - 87  
Bliem, Barbara - 34  
Blouch, J. H. - 95  
    Johann - 24  
    Joseph - 9  
    Rosanna - 47  
Boas, Henry - 10  
    Jeremiah - 92  
    Magdalena - 10  
Bobb, Chambers - 88  
Boeshor, Thomas - 39  
Boeshore, Amanda - 45  
    Elisabeth - 6  
    John Henry - 81  
    Josua - 80  
    Lewina - 12  
    Samuel - 38  
    Sebilla - 18  
    William - 63  
Boger, Essie - 79  
    John A. - 65  
    Mary Ann - 93  
    Thomas - 62, 76  
Bollack, John - 90  
Bollinger, Henry - 11  
Bollman, Jacob - 15  
Bolton, Johannes - 88  
Boltz, Edmund T. - 76  
    Louisa - 96  
    Maria - 14  
    Mary Ann - 76  
    Stephen W. - 61  
    William - 89  
Bolz, John - 23  
    Relena - 31  
    Samuel - 26  
    Sarah - 42  
Bomberger, Christian S. - 69  
    Irael - 82  
    Jacob - 16  

Bomberger, John S. - 13  
    Joseph - 77  
    Kate - 77  
    Sarah - 28  
Bonawitz, Sarah - 31  
Books, M. Washington - 18  
Border, John H.  
Borry, John - 92  
Borgner, John - 23  
Bossler, Sarah L. - 77  
Bowman, Joanna - 74  
    Louis - 96  
Boyer, Amanda - 54  
    Benjamin - 14  
    Daniel - 16  
    Elisabeth - 44  
    John A. - 74  
    Joseph - 97  
    Leah - 21  
    Lodia - 53  
    Maria E. - 90  
    Melinda Henrietta - 59  
    Moses - 48  
    Solomon - 92  
Brand, Johannes - 63  
    Maria - 38  
Brandt, Abraham - 64  
    Daniel - 87  
    Emma G. - 44  
    Isaac - 87  
    John - 53  
    Maria - 59  
    Martin - 41  
    Mary - 67  
    Rosanna - 72  
Brant, Levi - 69  
Brauch, Maria Anna - 38  
Braumiller, Ester - 77  
    Maria - 55  
Braun, Amanda - 27  
    Andreas - 32  
    Catharina - 49  
    Christian S. - 82  
    David - 30  
    Elisabeth - 27  
    Friederich - 24  
    John - 47  
    Margareth - 16  
    Maria - 85  
    Philip - 77  
Brechbill, Abraham - 87  
    Amanda - 72  
    Anna - 66  
    Catharina - 56  
    Joseph - 54

Brechbill, Joseph - 54
    Susanna - 66
Brehm, Matilda - 55
Breitenbach Eliada E. - 44
Breitigain, Elisabeth - 42
Brenner, Peter - 90
Breslin, William J. - 13
Bretz, Lydia Ann - 51
    Susanna - 73
Bretzius, Salome - 20
Bricker, Aaron - 93
    Jacob - 44
    Magdalena - 78
    William - 28
Brooks, Eliza - 3
Bross, John Henry - 45
Brossman, George - 50
    Jacob - 7
Brotherlein, Charles - 40
Brough, Hanna - 7
    Heinrich - 33
Brown, Aaron - 29
    Susannah - 83
Brubacher, Catharina - 13
    Elizabeth - 71
    Jacob - 70
    Joel - 83
    Margaret Ann - 89
    Mary Ann - 41
    Peter - 86
Bruch, David - 74
Brunner, Louisa - 36
    William E. - 87
Buch, Henry - 58
Bucher, Peter - 79
    Samuel R. - 5
Buchmoyer, Jane - 50
Buchter, Catharina - 81
    Elias - 22
    Samuel - 44
    Sarah Anna - 71
Buck, Mary - 8
Buffington, Polly - 80
Burkhart, Eva - 93
    Malinda - 85
Burkholder, Catharina - 93, 94
    John - 8
    Leah - 54
    Michael K. - 57
    Samuel - 57
    Susanna - 55
Burky, Sophia - 72
Burnside, William J. - 16, 27
Buschong, Jacob - 5

Caldwell, Anna - 62
Campbell, John - 73 (2)
Care, Hannah - 12
Carl, Elisabeth - 41
Carmany, Christopher - 46
    John G. - 18
Carmony, Leah - 9
    Lucetta - 17
Carpenter, Susanna - 35
Carper, Sarah Ann - 44
Carry, Angelina - 17
Carver, Elisabeth - 8
Cassel, Sarah - 32
Cassidy, Malinda - 21
    Pharis - 21
Christ, Anna - 38
    Catharina - 10, 79
    Elisabeth - 34
    Mary - 74
    Nathan - 91
Christman, Catharina - 64
Clark, Michael - 83
    Walter - 34
Claus, John - 36
Clay, Elizabeth - 96
    Leah - 42
Clemens, Catharina - 43 (2)
Clendenin, Anna E. - 75
    Cosmus - 67
Colder, James - 16
Coleman, Harriet - 11
    James - 11
Coller, Cyrus - 82
Conner, Henry - 33
Conrad, Catharina - 55
    James - 2
Conran, James - 5
Cooper, Milton - 19
    Rosanna - 47
Corl, Levi - 60
Corner, Rosyann - 26
Corry, Barbara -29
Cox, Anna - 5
    Henry - 47
    Mary - 49
Craiglow - 26
Craiglow, David - 49
Cramer, Peter M. - 83
Crick, Mary Ann - 58
Cunard, Leah - 91
Dall, Ellen - 22
Daniel, Sarah - 43 (2)
Darkes, Margaret - 52 (2)
Daub, Catharina - 75

Daub, Elisabeth - 1
    John - 19, 20
    Joseph - 64
    Malinda - 82
    Sarah - 37, 56
Daubert, George - 31
Daugherty, Jeremiah E. - 54
Davis, Charles - 62
Deck, Elisa - 29
    Jacob - 49
    John - 53
    Lea - 86
    Melinda - 71
Degler, Daniel - 72
DeHart, Caroline - 8
    Rebecca - 24
Deininger, Lavina Anna R. - 58
    Polly - 75
    Samuel - 55
Demler, Christian - 63
Dengler, Polly - 44
Denlinger, Amos - 27
Deppen, Matilda - 28
Derkes, Adam - 79
    Henry - 45
    John - 14
    Samuel K. - 62
    Tobias - 61
Derr, Charles - 32
    Margaretha - 71
    Maria F. - 92
    Purmilla - 50
Desch, Lavina - 10
Detweiler, Samuel - 44
Dibbel, Fianna - 85
Dickel, Daniel - 24
Dieben, Peter - 94
Dieffenbach, William - 5
Diehl, Samuel - 56
Diehl, widow - 46
Diemer, Henry - 60
    John - 62, 63
Diener, Amos - 95
Dietrich, John - 18
Dillman, Mary - 95
Dinges, Lydia - 59
Dissinger, Cyrus - 93
    Edward - 44
    Mary - 70
    Sarah - 54
Ditzler, George W - 6
    Isaac - 72
    Lydia - 76
    Maria Anna - 50

Dixon, Elizabeth - 64
Dohner, Henry - 35, 93
    Joseph - 35
    Mary - 94
Dollinger, Rebecca - 11
Dollum, Henry - 80 (2)
Dondeur, Friederich - 89
Dondor, Samuel - 3
Donemeier, Johannes - 13
Donley, Ann - 91
    Fanny - 60
    John - 36
    Sarah - 22
    William - 63
Donmeier, Devilla - 79
Donmeyer, Lewis - 94
Donmoyer, Angeline - 76
    Franklin - 43
    Josiah - 66
    Ruben - 94
Donnenberger, Eliza - 95
Dornbach, Elisabeth - 2
Dotter, Caroline - 78
    David S. - 71
Dow, Mary A. - 64
Drayton, William Howard - 11
Dreist, Catharina - 94
Dubbs, Rosanna - 87
    Susan - 53
Dubs, Catharina - 56
    Isaac - 18
    Jacob - 17
    Jonathan - 59
    John - 17
    Malinda - 43
Duppel, Sarah - 95
Duth, Edwin Carl - 68
Dutter, Abraham - 44
Dutweiler, Jacob - 65
    John - 74
Earley, Margaret - 34
Early, Daniel - 17
    Moses - 18
Eba, Edward - 25
Ebach, Wilhelmina - 12
Eberly, Elias - 50
    Isaac - 35
    Sarah - 80 (2)
    Susan - 3
Ebersole, Henry - 43
Ebert, Bellamina - 1
Ebrecht, Catharina - 43
    Susan - 64
Ebur, Thomas R. L. - 6

Eby, Ann - 15
   Catharina - 41, 79
   Henry W. - 68
Eckel, Maria - 37
Eckert, Daniel H. - 94
   George R. - 87
   Jacob - 83
   Samuel - 76
   William - 22, 70
Edris, Jacob - 87
Eggenroth, Mary Anna - 72
Ehler, Samuel - 20
Ehrman, Caroline - 91
Eisenhauer, Emanuel - 33
   George - 43 (2)
   Joseph - 50
   Mary - 92
   Sarah - 3
   Susanna - 14
Eisenman, Johann - 41
Elder, Mary - 69
Ellenberger, Amende - 15
   Sarah - 83
Ellinger, Elizabeth, 69, 70
   Isaac - 65
   Kate M. - 92
   Lydia - 26
Elliot, David S. - 91
   Hannah - 1
Elliott, John Jr. - 62
Ely, Anthony S. - 39
   Elisabeth - 45
   George F. - 80
   John - 16
   Lavina - 16
   Matilda - 79
Embich, Andrew H. - 41
   Anna - 7
   Daniel - 31
   Louisa H. - 39
   Sarah - 66
   Susan - 19
   Wiliam H. H. - 66
Emerich, Sarah Ann - 74
Emrich, C. - 4
   David - 43
Enck, Sarah - 52
Endesberger, Rudolph - 58
Engel, Mary Elisabeth - 5
Engelhart, Henrietta - 25
English, Anna Elisabeth - 85
Ensminger, Anna M. - 13
   Lidia - 26
Epler, Daniel - 1

Epler, John L. - 78
Epling, John - 23
Erb, Sarah - 78
Ermel, Rebecca - 92
Eschelberger, Maria - 38
Eschliman, Christian - 16
   Sarah - 16
Etris, Elias - 57
   Henry - 29
   John - 29
   Matilda - 24
Ettendyer, John - 82
Etter, Gideon - 89
   Jacob - 15
Ettris, Lydia - 61
Evens, Jluianna - 35
Everett, John - 3
Eversole, Ann - 21
Evy, Mary - 74
Faber, Catharina - 57
   George M. - 54
   John - 95
   John M. - 78
   Mahlon - 20
   Samuel - 56 (2)
Fahnestock, Elisabeth - 27
   G. - 27
   Henry - 43
Fasnacht, Fayette - 90
   Rebecca - 97
   William - 53
Fassnacht, Maria - 88
Fausler, Rebecca - 91
Faust, Adam - 25
Federulf, Maria - 43
Fegan, Daniel - 45
Fegle, Lea - 10
Fehg, Rosina - 58
Feldy, Levi - 12
Felke, Michael - 95
Fellenbaum, Kate - 80
Felter, Samuel - 30
Felty, Eliza - 5
   Maria - 60
   Susannah - 33
Fenstermaker, Elisabeth - 26
Fernsler, Polly - 57
   Rebecca - 32
Ferry, Elisabeth - 24
Fesig, Johann - 57
Fessler, Eliza - 69
   John P. - 74
   Reuben - 79
   Sarah - 22

Fessler, Sarah - 22, 50
Fetter, Edward - 51
    Henry- 37
    Levi - 81
Field, John - 91
Fieman, David - 54
    Eliza - 3
Fies, Catharina - 35
    Josia - 90
    Josiah - 90
    Samuel - 42
Fiess, Jeremiah - 68
    Mary - 26
Filbert, Eli - 89
    Franklin - 10
    Isabella - 89
Fink, Catharina - 82
Fisch, Lewis - 91
Fischer, Carolina - 44
    Catharina - 15
    Elvina - 29
    Henry - 91
    Lawina - 39
    Ludwig Jr. - 59
    Luther - 33
    Maria - 6
    Mary - 95
    P. - 74
    Samuel L. - 92
    Sophia - 12
    Thomas - 3
    William L. - 75
Fischhorn, Joseph - 1
Fitterer, Elisabeth - 44 (2)
Fitting, Elisabeth - 89
Flagg, Henry - 42
Flitsch, Margaret - 78
Flory, Jane A. - 41
Flower, Herman - 28
Flowers - 10
Focht, Catharina - 21
    Conrad C. - 23
    William - 4
Folmer, Hannah - 58
Foltz, Friedrich - 55
    Henry - 78
    Susan - 62
Ford, David G. - 14
Foreman, Abraham - 57
    Hannah - 62
Forney, Barbara - 28
    Henry - 26
    Josephine - 36
    Lydia H. - 27

Forney, Samuel - 87
Fornwald, Jacob - 90
Fornwalt, Elisabeth - 74
    John - 35
Forrer, Cyrus - 36
    Isaac - 2
    Jonathan - 51
Forry, Mary - 10
    Mary Ann - 29
    William - 27
Fortna, Lydia Ann - 18
    John H. - 74
Fox, Aaron - 44
    Amanda - 24
    Catharina - 72
    John - 91
    Lucinda W. - 67
    Mary - 27
    Rachel - 32
    Richard - 30
    Rosanna - 89
    Sara - 93
    Susan - 93
Foy, William - 22
France, Ann Caroline - 91
Francis, Jacob K. - 44
Frank, Henry - 12
Frankhouser, Cathariana - 50
Frantz, Catharina - 92
Freiling, Johannes - 20
Freimoyer, Sarah - 14
Freylinghaus, Ellen Johanna - 81
    Peter H. - 56
Fritz, John H. - 85
Fronk, John - 67
Fry, Catharina - 54
Fuchs, Amos - 19
    Elisabeth - 60
    Gernelius - 43
    Joel - 23
    Johannes - 81
    Morris - 19
    Josiah - 37
    Martin - 30
    Mary A. - 2
    Sarah - 27
Fuss, John G. - 50
Gabel, Jacob G. - 88
Gackley, Susanna - 83
Gamber, Maria Anna - 80
Garber, Maria Ann - 45
Garberich, Mary - 95
Garberig, Tobias W. - 58
Garrett, Sarah - 71

Gasser, John - 38
    Levia - 29
    Samuel - 94
    William - 92
Gassert, Elisabeth - 33
    Jeremias - 67
    Mary - 10
    Sara Ann - 88
Gehres, Catharine - 76
Gehret, Johannes - 28
    Lodia - 54
    Sara - 68
Geib, Jonas - 79
Geiser, Levi - 89
    Peterine - 94
Geiss, Catharina - 78
    Melinda - 20
Gelbach, William - 22
Gelebach, Harriet - 19
Gelsinger, Philip - 49
Gembel, William - 45
Gemi, George - 67
Gensemer, Daniel - 89
George, Harriet S. - 68
Gerberich, Adnrew - 66
    David - 21
    Elias - 45
    Elias T. - 34
    Elisabeth - 94
    Henry S. - 42
    Joseph - 66
    Magdalena - 46
Gerdy, Susan - 69
Gerhard, Anthony - 83
    Elisabeth - 28
    Isaac - 53
    John - 2
    John P. - 82
    M. - 3
    Rebecca - 87
Gerhart, Anna M. - 74
    Catharina - 40
    Cornelius - 62
    Isaac - 75
    Jesse - 68
    Maria - 29
    Sarah Ann - 58
    Susanna - 53
Gerling, George - 68
Gerloff, Sarah - 50
German, Angeline - 36
    Susanna - 14
Gerret, Elisabeth - 87
    James - 60

Gerret, Mary - 32
    Peter - 79
    Sarah - 73
Gerrett, Andress - 1
Gerth, Susanna - 11
Gettel, Elisabeth - 30
    Malinda - 70
Getts, Elisabeth - 21
Getz, Catharine - 69
    Jacob - 61
    John - 84
Gier, Mary A. - 94
Giesey, Henry - 54
    Jacob - 36
Gilbert, Eliza - 7
Gingerich, David B. - 76
Gingerich, Isaac - 76
    Magdalena - 19
Gingrich, Christian K. - 28
    David - 76
    David B. - 27
    Elisabeth - 3
    Isaac - 13
    Joseph - 26
    Mary Ann - 61
Ginter, Leah - 58
Gippel, Joseph P. - 73
    Moses - 83
Glick, Elisabeth - 55
    George - 84
    Heinrich - 20
    Mary Anna - 42
Gloninger, Cyrus - 15
Gockley, Catharina Ann - 13
    Jacob - 54
    Peter - 54
    Sarah - 12
Goff, Gordon R. - 41
Goldman, Isaac - 12
Good, Mary - 65
Goodman, Elisabeth - 30
    G. W. - 36
Gordon, Elisabeth S. - 13
    James - 13
Goschert, Lizzie S. - 39
    Susan Matilda - 59
Gossert, Georg - 94
Gottschall, John - 77
Gotwalt, Eliza - 68
Graby, Barbara - 35
Grate, Joel - 60
Graff, Henry - 15
Graiglow, John - 19
Gratz, John - 58

Graybill, Jacob - 34  
Greenblatt, Maria - 94  
Greims, Susanna - 8  
Gress, Catharina - 58  
Gretscher, Andreas - 80  
Grittinger, Adam - 6  
    Lucretia M. - 6  
Groff, Anna M. - 74  
    Anna Maria - 30  
    Michael -55  
    Samuel S. - 88  
    Susanna - 53  
Groh, Elisabeth - 16, 73  
    Jacob - 73  
    John - 16  
    Levi J. - 92  
    Michael - 55  
    Peter - 13  
    Sarah - 27  
    William H.  
Grohman, Maria - 24  
Grove, Moses - 65  
Gruber, Catharina - 38  
    Elisabeth Ann - 44  
Gruber, Israel - 36  
    John - 37  
Grumbein, Catharina - 18  
    Susanna - 11  
Guth, Catharina - 22  
Grumlauf, Catharina - 68  
Guilford, W. Moore - 69  
Gundreman, John - 71  
Gundrum, Matilda - 59  
    Rebecca - 86  
    Sarah - 53  
Cuth, Catharina - 56 (2)  
    Christian - 77  
    Maria - 55  
    Rebecca - 50  
Haagte, Sophia - 82  
Haak, Jerome - 93  
    John - 44 (2)  
    Louisa - 32  
    Sarah Ann - 69  
    Solomon - 79  
Hacker, Ann - 15  
    J. - 11  
    Louisa - 87  
Hackman, Frances - 48  
Hagi, Catharina - 59  
Hagy, Moses - 25  
Hain, Albert - 74  
    Isaac - 83  
Hall, Anna M. - 88  

Hallman, Samuel - 7  
Halter, Helen L. - 39  
Haman, C. S. - 93  
Hambleton, Franklin - 78  
    Herman J. - 66  
Hamilton, Cyrus - 48  
Hammer, Catharina - 61  
    Elijah - 21  
    Mary A. - 21  
    Rebecca - 46  
Hammond, Catharine - 75  
    R. H. - 75  
Hanefius, Matilda - 25  
Harbeson, Amanda - 77  
    Samuel - 77  
Hare, John - 70  
Harner, Sarah - 83  
Harnish, Samuel - 37  
Harper, H. C. - 21  
    Henrietta - 1  
    Thomas - 1  
    Thomas H. - 76  
    Wilhelmina - 12  
Hartlein, Ellen - 63  
    Nathaniel - 17  
Hartman, Albert - 95  
    Amelia - 89  
    Amilia - 94  
    David - 95  
    Elvina - 89  
    George Henry - 46  
    Joseph - 91  
    Mary - 51  
    Sarah Ann - 60  
    William - 12  
    Wilmina - 60  
Hassinger, Henry - 11  
Hassler, David - 77  
    Elisabeth - 18  
Hauck, Daniel - 3  
    Samuel - 40  
    Sarah - 87  
    Sarah H. - 40  
Hauer, Isaac - 85  
    Levi - 49  
    Maggie - 85  
    Sarah - 24  
Hauert, Sarah - 22  
Haughy, Jacob - 76  
Hauk, Adam - 55  
Hauscht, Angelius - 82  
Hauts, Eliza - 17  
    Mary - 95  
    Samuel - 86

Hawk, Lovina - 53
Hay, George - 71
Hean, Albert A. - 74
    R. - 49
Heberling, Elisabeth - 15 (2)
Heck, Lavina - 85
Heckman, Thomas - 84
Hedrich, Jacob - 63
    Mary - 69
Heffelfinger, Cyrus - 23
    Edward - 46
Heffner, Kate M. - 75
Hege, William - 62
Hegele, John - 58
Hegy, Henry - 87
    John - 8
Heilman, Amelia - 87
    Benjamin - 88
    Daniel - 64
    Elisabeth - 46
    Henry - 52
    Jacob - 85
    Joseph - 97
    Levi - 21
    Parmilla - 60
    Reuben - 67
Heim, Jacob - 24
Heinege, John - 83
Heinly, Polly - 67
Heintzelman, Andrew - 79
Heisey, John H. - 91
Heisy, John S. - 42
Helder, Amanda - 85
    John - 78
Helm, Rebecca - 81
Helwig, John - 22
Helwood, Isabella - 23
Hemperly, Adam - 45
    George - 69
    Henry - 31
    Jacob F. - 67
Henning, Amanda - 46
    Daniel - 19
    Elisabeth - 36
    George - 54
Henninger, George - 63
Henry, Abraham - 11
    Andrew R. - 28
    Eliza - 25
    John - 86
    Sara - 5
Herbst, Joseph - 36
Herchelroth, John - 82
Hergelroth, Eva - 37

Herman, Philip - 26
Herr, Abraham - 89
    Daniel - 5
Herring, David - 18
Herschberger, Daniel - 56
    Henry - 58
    Johannes - 48
    Magdalena - 14
Herschey, Elisa - 14
    Henry - 52
    John - 52
    Susan - 91
Herzler, Leah - 11
Hess, Amende - 17
    Carolina - 27
    Elisabeth - 45
    George - 7
    John - 11
    Magdalena - 66, 87
Hetrich, David - 78
Hetz, Mary - 94
Hibschman, Jacob - 28
    John - 56
    John P. - 90
Hiestand, Jacob L. - 72
High, Jacob - 38
Himmelberger, Benjamin - 28
    George - 82
    Mary - 17
Hirchle, John - 82
Hittle - 31
Hittle, Mary A. - 31
Hitz, George - 31
Hixenheiser, Caroline - 33
Hochstetter, Daniel - 28
Hoffa, Levi - 75
Hoffer, Catharina - 8
    George - 89
    Mary - 85
Hoffert, Benjamin G. W. - 11
    Rosanna - 95
    Susanna - 42
Hoffman, Francis - 76
    George W. - 90
    Joel - 16
    John - 61
    John N. - 63
    Josephine - 54
    Tobias - 10
Hoke, Henry - 20
    Mary - 67
    William - 7
Holdri, Esther - 12
Hollinger, Elizabeth - 70

Hollinger, Fanny - 11
    Mary Ann - 82
Holsberg, Catharine - 65
Holsem, Helena - 62, 63
    Maria - 63
Homer, George - 72
Holzstein, John - 1
Hoover, Catharina - 28
    L. - 92
    Mary - 92
Horn, Washington - 81
Hornberger, Henry - 94
Hornefius, Lydia - 10
    Susan - 85
Horst, Catharina - 2
    Elisabeth - 66
    Joseph - 86
    Michael - 69, 70
Horstich, conrad - 75
Hortnent, Catharina - 64
Hostetter, Abraham - 65
    Eliza - 55
    Henry - 7
    John - 12
    Lydia - 9
    Mary - 65
    Nancy - 7
    Phrene - 21
Houtz, Henry - 53
Howard, Anna - 72
Hower, George - 11
    Isaac - 84
    Maggie - 84
Huber, Susanna - 17
Hugh, David - 54
Hughes, Buschrod W. - 41
    David - 81
    Montgomery - 57
Hummel, Benneville - 43
    Heinrich - 20
    Louisa - 12
Hunsberger, Maria - 30
Hunsicker, Carolina - 13
    David - 16, 30
    Elisabeth - 72
    Jacob - 78
Huntsberger, Samuel S. - 83
Huntzinger, George - 33
Huy, Jane - 96
Ibach, Sara - 93
Ihrig, Leah - 28
Illig, Katharina - 5
Imboden, Adam - 9
Immel, Mary Ann - 32

Ingle, Benjamin M. - 16, 17
Ingham, John - 48
    William S. - 84
Ingrum, Catharina - 37
Ives, Edward D. - 37
Irisch, Theodore - 21
Jacoby, Elisabeth - 87
Jennings, Lewina - 52
John, Ellen - 4
Jones, John - 17
Jung, Sarah - 16
    Sarah Ann - 77
Jury, George - 34
Justen, Johannes E. - 71
Kahlbach, Diana - 45
Kain, George W. - 61
Kapp, George - 68
    Levi - 95
Karch, John K. - 68
Karl, Daniel - 67
Karmany, Jeremiah - 48
Karmeny - 44
Karra, Samuel - 42
Karry, Catharine - 16
Kasper, Alois - 94
Kassel, Jacob - 90
Katz, Carolina - 27
Kauffman, Catharina - 95
    Joseph - 63
Kaufman, Anna - 3
    Catharina - 24
    Henrietta - 48
    Jacob - 31
    Johannes - 62
    Susannah - 94
Keath, Cyrus - 70
    Elisabeth - 76
Keen, Elisabeth - 9
Keener, Magdalena - 17
Kehl, Isaac R. - 58
    John P. - 62, 63
    Maria - 25
Keim, Mary L. - 62
Keiser, Amelia A. - 69
Kelchner, Emilie - 86
    Fianna - 34
Keller, Daniel - 4, 40
    David C. - 38
    Ellen - 88
    Jacob - 70
    Johannes - 39
    Mary - 4
    Nancy - 89
    Sarah - 6

Kelly, John - 14
Keltner, Margaret - 20
Kemmerer, Heinrich - 38
Kercher, David - 9
    Elisabeth - 52
Kerchner, Adam - 56
    Lydia - 24
Kern, William - 48
Kessler, John - 75
    Josuah - 76
Kessling, Johanna Fredericka - 58
Kettering, Eliza - 65
Ketterline, Mary - 10
Keifer, John - 50
Kieffer, Daniel - 3
Kiener, Catharina - 88
    Elisabeth - 85
Kienpatz, Elisabeth - 1
Kieser, Daniel - 90
Killian, Mary - 20
Killinger, DAvid - 54
    Elisabeth - 40
    John W. - 31
    Margaret - 48
    Rosa - 50
    Samuel - 48
    William F. - 8
Killmer, Jonathan H. - 71
Killwell, Elisabeth - 42
    John H. - 26
Kindig, Joseph - 89
Kinsey, John - 87
Kintzel, Lucetta - 79
Kinzel, Amanda - 6
Kipp, SAmuel - 12
Kircher, Christina - 28
Kiscadden, Catharina - 85
Kissinger, Henry - 83
Kitzmiller, Kate - 83
    Leah - 7
Klar, Daniel - 87
Kleimer, David - 53
Klein, Catharina - 61
    Daniel - 57
    Edward - 58
    Ester - 78
    George - 66
    Henry - 88
    Jacob - 11
    John - 11
    Joseph - 46
    Levi - 1
    Moses - 19
    Moses S. 70

Klein, Peter - 5
    Rebecca - 43
Kleinfelder, Maria - 25
Kleinfelter, John - 21
    Julianna - 89
    Leah - 81
Kleiser, Anna - 30
    John - 30
    Rosanna - 70
Klemenz, Wilhelmina - 28
Klick, John - 42
    John J. - 70
Klind, Sophia - 21
Kline, Mary - 18
Klingler, Samuel - 54
Klopp, Elias - 2
Klopp, Sarah - 84
    William - 91
Kniesel, Elisabeth - 31
    John - 17
    William - 56
Knoebel, Peter B. - 57
Knoll, Henry - 96
    Sarah - 15
Knox, Jane G. - 40
Koch, Friedrich - 41
    Hannah - 36
Kochenderfer, Catharina - 30
    Rosanna - 38
Kochler, Joseph - 24
Kohl, Catharina - 13
    John - 43
Kohr, John Heinrich - 68
    Maria Magdalena - 84
Kolb, Francis - 5
Koons, Jacob - 9
    Mary - 85
    Sarah Ann - 57
    Thomas - 56
Krall, Abraham - 71
    Amos - 13
    Catharina - 12
    Daniel - 89
    John - 46
    Rebecca - 76
Krater, William G. - 16
Kratzer, Jacob - 41
    Lusinda - 90
Krause, Priscilla - 31
Krebel, John - 69
Kreider, Catharina - 78, 83
    Elisabeth - 41, 58
    Jacob L. - 16
    Joseph - 86 (2)

Kreider, Joseph - 86 (2)
    Katharina - 71
    Levi A. - 82
    Mary - 70 (2), 93
    Mary A. - 81
    Michael - 70
    Sarah - 67
    Sarah Ann - 29
    William B. - 88
Kreiser, Anna Maria - 73
    Chris - 62
    Elias - 60
    Eliza - 61
    Magdalena - 21
    Maria - 30
    Sabina - 77
    Sarah - 94
    Thomas - 34
Kreitz, William F. - 77
Kreitzer, Michael C. - 31
Kremer, Israel - 19
    Joseph - 69
    Lodia - 64
    Lydia - 54
Kretzmoyer, Leah - 36
Krick, Jacob - 9
    John H. - 32
Krum, John R. - 66
Krumlauf, Samuel - 32
Krupp, Lidia - 49
Kuhnle, Mary A. - 65
Kuhns, Catharina - 29
    Maria - 38
    Mary A. - 83
Kunkel, John C. - 84
Kuntzelman, Anna - 87
Kupp, Henry - 90
Kurr, Elisabeth - 22
    Rebecca - 71
Kurtz, Conrad - 12
    Elisabeth - 27
    John - 89
    Levi - 15
    Mary - 77
    Sarah - 55
Kurz - 10
Lab, Sarah - 10
Lamp, Catharina - 92
Landis, Catharina - 39
    David - 74
    David K. - 26
    Frances N. - 18
    Henry - 56
    Hiram F. - 72

Landis, Maria E. - 29
    Mary - 58, 72
    Nancy - 88
    Rebecca - 22
    Sarah - 14
Lang, David - 74
    George - 6
    Jacob - 55
    Joseph - 73
    Samuel - 46
Lantz, Catharina - 90
    Eliza - 90
    George - 43
    Johannes - 1
    John - 38
    Sarah A. - 71
Lasch, Emanuel - 56
    Sarah - 66
Lascomb, William H. - 40
Lau, Maria - 17
Laucks, Eva - 91
Lauden, William - 94
Lausch, William - 93
Lauser, Carolina - 23
    George - 23
    Joseph - 56
Lautenschlager, Maria - 36
Lautermilch, Anna Maria - 1
Law, Levi - 3
Lawery, Phrany - 19
Leadum, susan - 67
Lease, Emmaline - 63
Lebengood, Malinda - 39
Lebenguth, Lewis A. - 89
Lebo, Isabella A. - 76
    William - 29
Lechner, Catharina - 3
    Mary - 27
Leffler, Rebecca - 58
Lehman, Abraham - 64
    David - 12
    Jacob - 35
    Levi - 49
    Samuel - 80
    Samuel B. - 30
    Sara Ann - 87
    Sarah - 27
Lehr, James D. - 61
Leinbach, Elmina M. - 3
    Joseph A. - 69
    Sarah Magdalena - 52
    T. H. - 52
Leineweber, George - 15
    Henry - 67

Leineweber, John - 23
Leininger, George - 35
    John - 47
    Sophia - 18
Lintner, Carolina - 57
Leitzel, Washington - 7
Lemmer, Emeline - 93
Lengel, Catharina - 87
    Michael - 29
    Paul - 55
Lentz, Jacob - 56
Leob, Levi - 27
Lerch, Benneville - 27
    Caroline - 70
    Cyrus - 83
Lescher, Maria Anna - 31
Lessley, Joseph - 82
    Mary - 70
    Susan B. - 69
Lesster, John - 43
Levengood, Lucy - 82
Licht, Abraham - 28, 65
    Adam - 49
    Amelia - 41
    Asaph - 61
    Elias R. - 71
    Elisabeth - 26, 30, 62, 65, 88
    Jacob C. 78
    John - 55
    Mary - 70
    Polly - 22
    Rosanna - 41
    Samuel - 19
    Sarah - 81
    Sarah E. - 32
    Solomon -13
Light, Felix - 5
    Felix B. 53
    Gideon - 31
    Israel - 38
    Jeremiah - 1
    Joseph G. - 33
Lindenmuth, George - 59
    Matilda - 18
    Sarah - 7
Lingle, Henry - 70
Lingel, Priscilla - 56
Litsch, Elisabeth - 2
Liveringshaus, Sarah - 34
Lob, Emilie - 42
    John - 42
    Moritz - 41
Lohr, Eva - 31

Long, Anna Mary - 80
    David - 14, 26
    Ephia - 42
    John - 36
    Lucy Ann - 25
    Reuben -59
Longenecker - 46
Longenecker, Anna B. - 83
    Barbara - 52
    John - 52
    Magdalena S. - 83
    Maria - 1
Loos, Catharina - 89
    Tobias - 45
Loose, Catharina - 32
Loser, Jonathan - 57
    William - 52
Louch, John - 68
Lowery, Elisabeth - 14
    Amanda E. - 82
Lowry, Eliza -79
Luckenbill, Rebecca - 64
Ludwig, Peter F. - 6
    Sebilla - 6
Lutz, Carolina - 10
    Daniel - 65
    George - 55
    Henry - 82
    John - 85
    Sarah - 7, 90 (2)
    Susanna - 59
Lynch, Susannah - 84
Mace, Jacob H. - 78
Madder, Abraham - 46
Majer, John - 54
Malleck, Maria - 95
Malm, Lea - 95
Malthar, Elisabeth - 6
Malvern, Carolina - 75
Manbeck, Sophia - 95
Mann, John W. - 90 (2)
Mark, Jane Eliza - 86
Markey, Samuel - 68
Markly, Anna E. - 5
Marks, Elias - 86
Marquart, Henry - 24
Marschall, Bell - 37
    Emeline - 37
    John G. - 37
Mart, Amanda - 19
Martin, Henry - 66
    William - 20
Martz, Johann - 40
Mathues, Anna - 60

Mathues, Anna - 60
Matis, Maria - 2
Matter, Elisabeth - 44
    Samuel - 7
Mattes, Joseph - 91
    Lovina - 81
Matthew, Solomon - 78
Matthews, Anna - 51
Matz, Joseph H. - 49
Maulfair, Elijah - 67
    Elisa - 38
    Levi - 65
    Susanna - 20
Maurer, Catharina - 53
Mautz, John -64
Maury, Catharina - 13
    Rebecca - 4
Mays, Elisabeth - 39
M'Cauley, C. D. - 10
McClemmings, Elisabeth - 42
McCloud, Julianna - 23
McConnell, Casper - 60
    Susan - 74
M'Cormick, Rebecca - 29
M'Curty, Sarah Jane - 59
McFearling, Levi - 80
McGarveg, Christopher - 88
McGinley, William - 94
McGowan, Alexander - 77
McKinney, Daniel - 85
    Moses - 8
McLahe, Hannah C. - 70
    Thomas - 70
McLane, Sarah Ann - 4
McLaughlin, George - 45
    Henry - 25
McPherson, G. - 16
Measss, Sarah - 28
Meck, Louisa - 65
    Susanna - 56
Mecklindy, Maria - 27
Mees, Mary - 7
    Tobias - 6
Meier, Anna - 79
    Delila - 56
Meiley, Elisabeth - 36
Meily, Charles - 17
    Elisabeth - 1
    Jacob - 66
    John - 39
    Mary - 19
    Sophia - 20
Meiser, George - 15
    Sarah - 93

Mell, Catharina Ann - 75
Mellinger, George W. -79
    Samuel E. - 37
    Susanna - 6
Mengel, Louisa - 76
Mentzer, Allen W. - 85
Merk, Cyrus - 89
    Cyrus K. - 92
    Sarah - 89
Mertz, Henry - 66
    Wilhelm - 61
Metz, Eliza - 87
Meyer, Carl - 94
    Christian - 15
    Daniel - 19
    Johann - 24
    Joseph - 9
    Levi - 24
    Rebecca - 1
    Susanna - 19
Meyers, William - 27, 73
M'Gee, John - 52
Mies, Cyrus - 58
    Henry - 90
Miess, Catharina - 81
    Jonathan - 73
    Lea - 20
    Priscilla - 63
    Solomon - 21
Miesse, Catharina Anna - 61
Miller, Abrm - 19 (2)
    Ann - 85
    Archibald - 4
    Carolina - 51, 83
    Catharina - 8, 67
    David G. - 30
    Edwin - 69
    Elisabeth - 2
    Eliza - 58
    Elizabeth Ann - 74
    Emanuel - 93
    Henry - 47
    Henry W. - 61
    Isaac - 11
    Jacob - 64
    Jacob W. - 39
    Johann - 5
    John - 60, 66, 82
    Jonathan - 33
    Joseph - 86
    Josua - 13, 72
    Leah - 29
    Louisa - 56
    Lovinia - 10

Miller, Magdalena - 19
    Maria - 47
    Maria Anna - 58
    Mary - 73 (2)
    Mary Ann - 66
    Nancy - 50
    Peter - 21
    Rebecca - 41, 73
    Rebecca Ann - 22
    Rosanna - 12, 38
    Samuel - 63
    Sara Anna G. - 68
    Sarah - 50, 86
    Solomon - 41
    Sophia - 62, 63
    Susanna - 2, 91 (2)
    William - 37, 74
Minnig, Cyrus - 65
Misch, P. B. - 75
Mischler, Henry - 45
Missimer, Henry - 57
    William M. - 12
M'Kinney, Maria - 72
    Samuel - 33
M'Kinny, Rebecca - 33
Mock, George - 26
Moltz, George - 19
Mooney, Benjamin - 4
Moore, Elijah - 32
    Henry - 85
    William - 52
Mordock, Sarah - 76
Morer, Catharina - 8
Mosser, Sara - 7
Moyer, Abraham - 36
    Adam - 6
    Catharina - 39
    Charles P. - 67
    Christina - 29
    David - 85
    Elisabeth - 41, 86
    Elmina - 15
    George N. - 53
    John - 10
    John G. - 92
    John W. - 90
    Lea - 10
    Leah - 86 (2)
    Lucetta - 35
    Lydia - 89
    Maria - 1
    Mary - 37
    Mary Ann - 36
    Peter - 37

Moyer, Rebecca - 25
    Sarah - 12
    Washington - 14
    William - 22
    William A. - 7
    William W. - 92
Mullen, Monroe H. - 60
Mummaw, Mary Ann - 69
Murdock, Amanda H. - 81
    Sarah - 77
Murrey, William - 29
Murry, John - 67
Muschler, Jacob - 51
Muth, Jefferson - 69
    Maria Ann - 21
    R. H. - 84, 85
    Richard - 93, 94
Mutschler, Catharina - 19
    Elisabeth - 54
    Fianna - 10
Nace, Catharine - 16
Nachtsinger, Nancy - 7
Nafzger, Clarisa - 67
    Michael - 10
Naftzinger, Hannah - 48
    Joseph - 14
Nagel, Rebecca - 86
Nagel_oner, Peter - 47
Nagle, John - 91
Nase, Andreas - 78
Negley, Emma L. - 19
Ness, Sarah - 26
Neu, Carolina - 63
    Samuel - 31
Neugardt, Lorenz - 17
Newman, Adam - 3
Ney, Adam - 14
    John - 86
    Regina - 77
    Samuel - 77
Nine, Mary - 90
Nitrauer, Jacob - 75
Noll, Adam - 67
    Catharina - 34
    Cyrus - 34
    Elisabeth - 43, 85
    Henry - 12, 25
    Isaac - 44
    Jacob - 37
    Joseph - 10
    Michael - 50
    Zadock - 3
North, Margaretha - 69
Noun, William - 58

Noun, William - 58  
Null, Leah - 31  
Numan, Rebecca - 47  
Nye, John - 86  
Ober, Frenica - 49  
Oberly, Caroline - 33  
O'Brien, Jackson - 48  
Ochs, William - 86  
Ochsenreiter, Elisabeth - 48  
O'Connel, Thomas - 64  
Oswald, Eliza - 37  
    John Henry - 84  
Otzman, Josiah - 7  
Overholzer, Elisabeth - 25  
Oves, Sarah Ellen - 13  
    Theodore - 32  
Oxenreider, William - 59  
Pain, Levi - 13  
Paine, Mary - 32  
Palm, Catharina - 3  
    Cyrus - 21  
    David - 54  
Pannebecker, Johann - 47  
Parker, Annie C. - 63  
Patten, Rachel Ann - 30  
Patterson, Libbia A. - 64  
Pauer, Catharina - 43  
Peck, John F. - 38  
Pedre, Retesa - 37  
Peffley, Abraham - 50  
    Jacob - 57  
    Jerry - 96  
    Sarah - 46  
Peffly, Jacob - 34  
Peifer, Benjamin - 2  
Peiffer, Matilda M. - 33  
Peleger, J. G. - 41  
Pentikuf, Wilhelm - 13  
Person, Elisabeth - 95  
    Sarah R. - 82  
Peter, Amelie - 59  
    Benjamin - 69  
    John - 51  
    Joseph - 67  
    Rebecca - 9  
    Rose - 84  
Peters, Harriet - 5  
    Leah - 23  
Petree, Amanda - 53  
Pfautz, Henry - 67  
Pfeifer, Edward - 83  
Pflieger, John - 62, 63  
Philbi, Lydia - 78  
Philip, Michael - 2  

Philippi, Redosia - 91  
Phillippi, Sarah - 46  
Philippy, Catharina - 88  
Philips, Jacob - 32  
    Lydia - 45  
Phillippi, Catharina - 9, 34  
    George - 29  
    Jacob - 20  
Phreaner, Carl B. - 4  
    Daniel - 22  
Pickel, Peter - 86  
Plattenberger, Susan - 20  
Plaugh, Hannah - 18  
Poorman, Friederich - 34  
    Rebecca - 43  
Porter, Margaret - 4  
Pott, John - 15  
Preis, Eliza Ann - 78  
    George - 22  
    Henry - 24  
Price, Catharina - 89  
Preusy, Dorothy - 89  
Puhr, Esther - 58  
Quigley, Mary Ann - 48  
    Wesley - 27  
Quimbe, John B. - 47  
Raab, Solomon - 60  
Rab, Sarah - 30  
Rabb, Noah - 15  
Radabach, Rosanna - 87  
Rager, Samuel - 82  
Rahn, Mary Elisabeth - 7  
Ramler, Elisabeth - 54  
    Polly - 18  
Rank, Catharina - 82  
    Henriette - 36  
    Josiah H. - 87  
Rapp, Let - 30  
Rauch, John - 46, 93  
    Margaretta - 94  
    Maria Anna - 35  
Reats, John - 59  
Reber, Isaac - 53  
    J. L. - 3  
    John - 87  
    Lucetta - 2  
Rebert, Rachel - 93  
Rebock, Maria - 36  
Reckenberger, Jacob - 52  
Redford, George - 51  
Redsecker, George - 75  
Reed, Catharine - 69  
    Esra - 3  
Reese, Mary - 18

Reese, Mary - 18
Reichelderfer, Maria - 41
Reichman, Henry - 6
    Maria Margaret - 70
Reidel, Lucy Ann - 90
    Mary - 58
Reifein, Elisabeth - 6
    Jacob - 24, 75
    Lydia - 63
Reily, Mary - 78
Reinhard, Anna Maria - 6
    Elisabeth - 88
    George - 39
    Rosanna G. - 55
Reinhold, Susanna - 54
Reinoehl, Catharina Ann - 93
    Jonathan - 52
    Susanna - 36
    Tob. - 92
    Tobias - 19, 41
Reiser, Maria - 35
Reissner, Mary Ann - 52
    Sarah A. - 68
Reist, Barbara Ann - 57
    Elisabeth - 26
Reiter, Priscilla C. - 16
Resch, Elijah - 25
    Polly - 73
Reth, Peter - 49
Rex, George - 1
Reyer, Abraham - 3
Reynolsen, Michael - 71
Richards, Amelia - 9, 10
Richarson, William - 40
Riddel, Elias - 54
Riechard, Adam S. - 95
Riechert, Mary - 71
Ried, Isaac - 45
    John - 22
    Joseph - 89
    Sarah - 9
Riegel, Jacob - 72
Riehm, Henry - 46
    Lovina - 51
    Martha - 57
    Mary Ann - 31
Riem, Caroline - 65
    Catharina - 29
    Justina - 20
Ries, Sara Anna - 75
Rieth, Elmira - 61
    Isaac - 7
    Israel - 46
    Lavina - 26

Rieth, Martha - 2
Riethy, Maria - 92
Rip, Jacob - 37
Rise, Lizzie - 67
Ritschert, Eva - 49
    John - 47
    Lucetta - 49
    Rebecca - 57
Rittel, Adam - 79
    Allemina - 28
    Catharina - 93
    David - 68
    Isaac - 34
    Johannes - 66
    John H. - 91
    Joseph - 11
Ritter, Maria - 45
    Rebecca - 13
Roberts, Mary - 62
Rodearmal, Anna - 75
Rodel, William D. - 36
Rohland, Catharina - 55
    Edward - 27
    Elisabeth - 36
    Mary - 60
    Sarah S. - 14
Rohrer, William - 14
Romig, Abraham - 90
Rosenberger, Carl - 47
Ross, Andreas - 47
Roth, Henry - 91
    Josia - 56
    Rebecca - 27, 29
    Wilhelm - 23
Rotharmel, Elisabeth - 44
Rothermel, Josiah - 6
Roths, Matilda - 10
Royer, Anna - 11, 15
    Benjamin - 19
    Harriet - 35
    Jonathan - 2
    Joseph - 26
    Leah - 19, 40
Rudy, Anna - 86
    Caroline - 48
    John - 80
Ruh, Jacob - 23
Ruhl, Carolina - 31
    George - 59
Runkel, Elisabeth - 56
    John - 11, 12
    Lea - 92
    Rosanna - 11
Rupp, Sarah - 69

Rusley, Thomas - 16
Russell Thomas H. - 78
Ruth, Adam - 29
    George - 84
    Maria - 65
    Susanna - 51
Rutherford, Elizabeth C. - 84
    W. W. - 84
Sahm, Leah - 87
Salen, Angelina C. - 78
Sander, Lawrence - 77
Sanders, Elisabeth - 76
Sanderson, Isaac - 64
Sarge, Joseph F. - 74
    Mary Ann - 5
Sargent, Mary Ann - 24
Satazahn, Catharina - 48
Sattazahn, Adam - 58
    Amalia - 93
Sattazan, Subina - 40
Satezahn, John Addison - 71
Sattezahn, Elisabeth - 52
    Johannes - 50
    Leah - 63
    Peter - 64
Sauden, Lydia - 95
Sauers, John - 76
Sayler, Johannes L. - 81
    Joseph - 22
Saylor, Elizabeth - 67
Schaak, Mary - 91
    Philip - 87
Schade, Belinda - 40
    Franklin - 72
    Sellera - 72
Schadel, Eliza - 64
Schaeffer, John - 8
Schafer, Maria - 62
Schaffer, Catharina G. - 30
    Christian - 57
    Elisabeth - 15
    Henry - 1
    John - 10
    Levi - 8
    Louisa - 84
    Magdalena - 49
    Mary - 21, 34
    Philip - 48
    Samuel - 72
Schaffner, John - 17
    John F. - 65
Schakespeare, Mary Ann - 73
Schally, John - 70
    Lydia - 22

Schally, Magdalena - 71
    Peter - 41
Schaly, Adam - 38
Schank, Rosanna - 40
Schantz, Joseph - 50
Scharp, Anna - 46
Schaud, Catharina - 79
Schaud, John Heinrich - 31
Schauers, Emma - 49
Schay, Barbara - 60
    George - 37, 42
    John - 24
    William S. - 94
Sched, maria - 51
Scheetz, John - 80
Scheib, Leah - 20
Scheiner, John - 10
    Mary - 25
    Samuel - 85
    William - 86
Schell, David - 8
Schellenberger, John H. - 80
Schenk, Catharina - 30
    Henry - 16, 42
    Michael L. - 30
    Susanna - 13
Schepler, Sarah - 24
Scheppler, Rebecca - 45
Scherdel, Adelina - 43
Scherg, Hanna - 68
    Johann G. - 73
Scherk, Abraham - 69
    Casper - 74
    Catharina - 47
    Catharina Ann - 87
    Elisabeth - 72
    John - 96
    Moses - 84
Schertzer, William - 46
Schiffer, Catharina - 41
    Levi - 16
Schilling, Stevens - 64
Schimp, John - 87
    Maria - 35
Schindel, Elisabeth - 52
    John - 41
    Joseph O. - 30
    Sarah - 41
Schirk, John - 55
    John G. - 59
    Samuel U. - 21
    Sophia - 32
    William - 28
Schitz, Lydia - 60

Schives, Catharina - 91
Schmaltz, Ann Eliza - 59
Schmalz, Elmira - 37
Schmeltzer, Catharina - 77
Schmidt, Catharina - 87
    Cornelius - 45
    Elian - 38
    Leah - 82
    Maria - 55
    Susanna - 48
    William R. - 65
Schnabely, John - 24
Schnebely, Catharina - 57
    C. J. - 13
    Elisabeth - 97
    Mary - 88
    Simon - 82
    Susan - 79
    Veronica - 82
Schnebly, Joseph - 8
Schneider, Benjamin - 31
    Catharina - 61, 71
    Catharina A. - 35
    Daniel - 59
    Diana - 23
    Elisabeth - 15, 23, 33
    John - 4, 24, 77
    Leventina - 54
    Maria - 1, 34
Schnewley, Catharina - 31
Schnurly, Elisabeth - 40
Scod, Anna Elisabeth - 56
Scholl, Griffith H. - 78
Schoop, Civilla - 74
Schort, Polly - 24
Schott, Elmeina - 29
    Jonathan - 37
Schram, Margaret - 42
    Mary - 42
Schraum, George - 6
Schreckengast - 50
Schreckengast, John - 8
Schreiber, Kelumban - 87
Schrieber, Carolina - 82
Schroff, Henry - 70
Schrom, Samuel - 65
Schrop, Daniel - 30
Schucker, Maria - 64
    Mary Ann - 60
    Susanna - 34
Schuey, Elisabeth - 14
    Heinrich - 28
    Johann Henrich - 14
    John B. - 79

Schuey, Magdalena - 39
    Maria - 88
    Sarah - 14
Schuger, Rebecca - 33
Schuhmacher, Sarah - 83
Schul, Susanna - 66
    William - 43
Schultz, Mary Margaret - 6
    Sarah - 3
Schumacher, Jacob - 82
    Mary - 24
Schuster, John - 9
Schwanger, Henry - 25
    Susanna - 68
Schwartz, Carolina - 14
    Elisabeth - 35
    Elisabeth H. - 71
    Jacob - 93
Schwartzenner, Lydia - 50
Schwarz, Angelina - 57
    Benjamin - 10
    Prescilla - 55
Schweitzer, William - 15
Schwob, Henrietta - 28
    Solomon - 53
Schwoyer, Elmina - 77
Scott, Anna Barbara - 48
Scully, Ellen C. - 64
Seaman, Mary - 24
Seabold, Rosanna - 71
Seasholtz, Reuben L. - 85
Sebold, John - 4
Segner, Angelina - 34
Segner, George - 49
Seibert, Angelina - 89
    James - 72
    Jonathan - 83
    Mary - 88
    Rebecca - 25
Seidel, Henry B. - 47
Seider, Anna - 80
    George - 14
    John - 2
Seiders, Catharina Anna - 84
    Ellen - 79
    John - 78
Seltzer, Anna - 92
    Clara S. - 67
    Henry U. - 15
    Jacob - 62
    Leonard - 4
    Louisa - 37
    Mary - 74
    Matilda - 39

Seltzer, Matilda - 39
Senner, Catharina - 66
Seybert, Elisabeth - 48
Shade, Christian - 63
Shaw, Henry - 62
Sheets, Anna - 64
Shetler, William - 92
Shimp, Sarah - 4
Shirk, Elisabeth - 3
Shugar, Leah - 71
    Sarah Ann - 84
Siegrist, Annie E. - 65
    Elisabeth - 19
    Franklin - 81
    Hiram - 88
    Louisa - 54
Silly, Catharina - 35
Simenton, Rebecca L. - 94
Singel, Christian W. - 81
Slicher, Amanda - 22
Sloan, James - 13
Smith, Caroline - 5
    George - 17
    George P. G. - 77
    Henry - 31, 32, 44, 46
    Isaac - 48
    Jacob M. - 84
    John - 20, 59, 76
    John E. - 85
    Leah - 30
    Louisa - 31
    Rosanna - 16
    Sarah - 30
    W. - 12
Smitt, Josua - 39
Snavely, Ann Margaret - 96
    Catharine - 5
    Christian - 91
    Henry - 22
    Henry H. - 51
    Jacob - 3
    Maria - 71
Snoddy, Ellen G. - 70
    Mary - 73
Snoke, Elisabeth - 66
Snyder, Thomas - 68
Sonnen, David - 17
Sott, John - 15
Sower, Ellen Louisa - 90
Spaeth, Eliza - 80
Spahnst, Sarah - 97
Spang, Isaac - 2
    Peter - 11
Spangler, Benewell - 17

Spangler, David W. - 39
    Elisabeth - 81
    Jacob - 60
    Mary Anna - 69
    Sarah - 85
Spankuch, Daniel - 48
Spannuth, Emanuel - 28
    George - 55
Spath, Jonathan - 15
Spatz, Absalom - 3
Spayd, Michael - 45
Speck, Catharina - 77
Speitel, John - 7
Spengler, Henry - 40
    Ro. - 2
Spitler, Lydia Ann - 3
    Magdalena - 59
    William - 12
Spittler, Drusilla - 52
    Lavian - 91
Spohn, Henry - 19
    Sarah Ann - 53
    Susanna - 14
Springer, Jacob - 3
Stager, Abraham - 93
    Henry - 2, 36
    Lea - 16
    Mary Ann - 37
    Sarah - 3
Stahl, Leah - 16
Stands, Ruben - 29
Stanly, John - 31
    Sarah - 72
Stauch, Angelina - 25
Stauffer, Abraham - 9
    Catharina - 57
    Mary Ann - 88
Steckbeck, Joseph - 34
    Sarah - 17
Steffy, Benjamin - 80
Steger, Catharina - 24
Stehley, Mary - 87
Stehly, Amanda - 67
Stein, Carolina - 43
    Elizabeth - 8
    Elisabeth - 54, 81
    P. - 65
    Sabina Elisabeth - 90
    Solomon - 26
Steiner, Anna - 12
    Augustus - 19
    Enos - 56
    John H. - 87
    Sarah - 28

Steiner, William - 26
Steins, Adam - 23
    George - 81
Stephen, Agnes - 47
Stevenson, Jane - 35
Stewart. Leucetta - 2
    Uriah B. - 25
Stichler, Henry - 76
Stickel, Catharina - 11
Stiely, Isaac - 10
Stiles, Maria Anna - 56
Stober, Ann Juline - 38
    Mary - 12
Stock, Heinrich - 20
Stoever, John - 39
    Susan M. - 85
    William - 14
Stohler, Henry - 9
Stohr, Jonas - 52
Stover, Amelia - 28
    David - 72
    Mary - 65
    Rosanna - 79
    Tobias - 29
Stophel, John - 83
Stout, Harriet - 83
    Isaac - 69
Strack, Daniel - 12
    Jacob - 25
Streack, George - 56
Strauss, Catharina - 87
Strickler, Elisabeth - 7
    Henrietta - 13
    Mary Ann - 47
    Polly - 50
    Sarah - 61
    William - 42
Stroh, Amanda S. - 62, 63
    John Jr. - 17
    Rebecca - 49
Strohm, Rebecca - 89
    Susan C. - 82
    William - 75
Strohman, John - 23
    Stephen D. - 14
Stroman, Rebecca - 33
Strubenhauer, Catharina - 26
Stub, William - 33
Stuckey, Eliphas W. - 84
Stump, Carolina - 21
Stump, Charles - 83
    Kesiah - 68
Swartley, Aaron - 70
Taylor, Sallie - 96

Teis, Jonas - 67
Teiss, Andrew - 37
Temple, Sarah Ann - 33
Theis, Lea - 88
    Mary Ann - 78
Thierwachter, Rebecca - 3
Thoma, Johannes - 31
Thomas, Charlotte - 11
    John - 11
    Louisa - 15
Thompson, Anna Elisabeth - 33
    Sarah Ellen - 57
Thrash, William - 95
Tice, Andrew - 3
Tittel, Sabina - 11
    John - 51
Tittle, Amos - 71
Tobias, Daniel - 31
    William - 70
Trautman, Lydia - 28
    Philip - 29
Treist, Sarah - 71
Treite, Catharina - 24
Trimble, Charles - 74
Trostel, George - 8
Troutman, Elisabeth - 55
Troxel, Mary - 67
Trump, Elisabeth R. - 92
    John - 61
Uhler, Catharine - 76
    George - 64
    John H. - 83
    Levi - 18
Uhrich, Catharina - 82
    Daniel - 43
    John - 55
    Susanna - 91
    William - 46, 52
Uhrig, David - 38
Ulrich, Christopher - 23
    Daniel - 96
    Isaac - 65
    John W. - 49
    Heinrich - 24
    Lea - 81
    Maria - 49
Umbehacker, Susanna - 4
Umbenhend, Peter - 25
    Samuel - 9
Umberger, Barbara - 70
    Jacob - 74
    John - 10
    John P. - 30
    Jonas - 55

Umberger, Joseph - 29
    Levi - 48
    William - 33
Upp, Annie - 94
Urich, George Peter - 10
    Henry Y. - 96
    Louisa - 67
Van Reed, Rebecca - 65
Viehl, Levi - 13
Virler, Henry - 59
Wachter, Sarah - 64
Wagner, Daniel - 24, 44
    Elias - 50
    Elisabeth - 24
    Fanny - 61
    George - 18
    Hannah R. - 66
    Henry G. - 34
    Isaac - 29
    Jacob - 57
    John - 85
    John Jr. - 32
    Louisa - 17
    Magdalena - 45
    Maria - 5, 66
    Rebecca - 8
    Sarah - 22, 23, 46
Walborn, Caroline - 9
    Edward - 7
    Elijah - 38
    Elisabeth - 25
    Israel - 61
    John - 39
Wallmer, Christina - 6
    Daniel - 14
    Elisabeth - 55
Walmer, Amos - 22
    Catharina - 20, 46, 79
    Eliza - 31
    Johannes - 28
    Samuel - 27
    Simon - 43
Walsch, John - 6
Waltemyer, Henry - 71
Walter, Elisabeth - 72
    George - 94
    John - 20
    John B. - 69
    Jonathan - 2
    Joseph - 58
    Louise - 51
    Maria - 23
    Rebecca - 4
    Sarah - 13

Walter, Thomas - 15
Waltermartin, Savilla - 57
Walters, Margaret - 62
Ward, Israel G. - 70
    John - 52
    John H. - 72
    W. G. - 47
Warren, Emma - 76
Weaber, Jerome S. - 67
Weasy, Ann - 18
Webber, Absalom - 85
Weber, Adam - 1
    Daniel - 88
    David - 11
    Elisabeth - 51
    John - 26
    John Henry - 71
    Martha - 73
    Peter - 24
    Sarah Ann - 11
Webert, John - 30
Weidel, George - 20
    Sarah - 9
Weidman, Aaron - 89
    Gideon - 28
    Emanuel - 64
    George - 60
    Maria - 18
Weigley, Allen - 85
    Caroline - 85
Weik, Emanuel - 28
    Sara - 49
    Sarah - 19
Weil, Johann - 61
Weir, George U. - 32
Weirich, George - 97
    Peter - 62
    William - 59
Weis, Mary A. - 96
    Rebecca - 26
Weiser, Maria - 12
    Maria Elisabeth - 13
Weiss, Amanda - 50
    Catharine - 60
    Daniel - 34
    Lydianna - 81
    Maria - 38
    Sarah - 38
    William - 42
Weith, Mary - 19
Weitzel, Amilia - 75
Weltmer, Susan - 26
Wender, Catharina - 17
Wendling, Amende - 23

Wendling, David - 56
    Lydia - 14
    Mary - 48
Wenger, Catharina - 16
    J. F. - 41
    Leah - 83
Wengert, Jacob - 63
    Lydia - 51
Wenner, Elisabeth - 13
Wennerich, Regina - 34
Wenrich, Franklin - 84
    Sarah Ann - 91
Wentzel, Aaron - 13
Werner, David T. - 27
    Henry - 91
    Jonathan T. - 95
    Levi - 38
    William - 95
Wertz, Catharina - 11
Westenberger, Elisabeth - 76
    John - 1
    Joseph - 21
    Michael - 73
    Samuel - 1
Whike, William - 29
White, John - 75
    Mary A. - 31
    Samuel - 68
Wiegand, Heinrich - 81
Wieland, John B. - 45
Wiest, Christian - 9
Wiestling, J. - 9
    Mary Ellen - 9
Wike, William - 27
Wilhelm, Elisabeth - 2
    William - 54
Williams, Lydia - 75
    Susannah - 37
    William - 5
Wilson, Helen E. - 75
Wilson, William R. - 33
Wimberger, Elizabeth - 95
Winebrenner, Ellen G. - 16
    J. - 16
Winkelbleck, John - 6
Winmoyer, Maryanna - 72
Winter, Henry - 89
    Susan - 83
Witman, Ellen - 3
    Henry - 93
    John - 21
    Jonathan - 13
    Jos. - 87
Witmer, Abraham - 25

Witmer, Anna - 15
    Catharina B. - 38
    Elisabeth - 88
    Henry - 5, 35
Witmeyer, John - 4
    Mary - 68
    Nancy - 31
Witmyer, Edward - 35
Wittemeyer, Henrietta - 67
Wittenmeyer, Catharina - 53
Wittman, Jonathan - 12
Wittmeyer, Catharine - 9
Wittmeyer, Cyrus - 7
    Rosanna - 27
Wohlleder, Elias - 77
Wolf, Catharina - 8, 19
    Cyrus - 27, 85
    Daniel - 6, 78
    Elisabeth - 57, 68
    Hannah - 11
    Henry - 77
    Herman - 49
    Isaac - 18
    John - 41, 91
    Louisa - 82
    Matilda - 80
    Rebecca - 11, 40, 42
    Samuel - 11
    Wilhelm - 88
Wolfersberger, Elisabeth - 45
    John H. - 86
    John Henry - 86
    Levi - 38
    Louisa - 8
    Mary E. - 86 (2)
Womelsdorf, Catharina - 92
Worth, T. T. - 9
Wummer, Adam - 36
Xander, David - 2
    Jacob - 85
Yeager, Catharina - 4
    Mary A. - 57
Yeagley, Catharina - 33
    Daniel - 1
    Elisabeth - 34
Yerger, John - 10
Yingst, Catharina - 40, 93
    Cyrus - 53
    David - 94
    Isaac - 2
    Lydia A. - 79
    Marie - 47
    Peter - 51
    Sarah - 44, 90

Yingst, Wilhelm - 38
Yocum, Aaron -75
    James - 81
    Josuah - 50
    Samuel - 32
Yoder, Maria Anna - 84
Yordy, Elias - 45
    George - 17
    John - 26
    Joseph - 66
    Nancy - 13
Young, John - 36
Youtz, Eleanor - 35
Yeungst, Andrew - 71
    John - 27
Zartman, Lovina - 64
    Peter - 64
Zell, John H. - 11
    Susanna - 12
Zeller, Elisabeth - 53
    Eliza - 6, 82
    Henrietta - 10
    Henry - 82
    John - 3
    Lucetta - 55
    Michael - 75
    Susanna - 10
Zerbe, Edward - 10
    George - 88
    Leventine - 36
    Percivell - 82
    William H. - 57
Zerver, Louisa - 43
Ziebach, Jacob - 35
Ziegler, John - 21
    Maria - 19
    Mary Ann - 47
    Rebecca - 19
    Sarah - 61
Zimens, Louisa - 20
Zimmerman, Andreas - 58
    Carl - 53
    Daniel - 30
    Edward R. - 77
    Eliza - 59
    Henry - 29
    Lea - 90
    Leah - 34
    Mary - 78
    Mary Ann - 17
    Rebecca - 75
    Sarah - 20
    Susanna - 30
Zinn, John - 4

Zug, Catharina - 94
    David - 86
Zweitzig, Angelina - 81
Zweizig, Mary - 21
Zweyer, Elizabeth - 1

www.ingramcontent.com/pod-product-compliance
Lightning Source LLC
Chambersburg PA
CBHW060402090426
42734CB00011B/2227